A JERUSALEM ANTHOLOGY

A JERUSALEM ANTHOLOGY

Travel Writing
through the Centuries

Edited by
T.J. Gorton
Andree Feghali Gorton

The American University in Cairo Press
Cairo   New York

Exclusive distribution outside Egypt and North America by I.B.Tauris & Co Ltd.,
6 Salem Road, London, W2 4BU

Dar el Kutub No. 26185/16
ISBN 978 977 416 842 0

Dar el Kutub Cataloging-in-Publication Data

Gorton, T.J.
    A Jerusalem Anthology: Travel Writing through the Centuries / T.J.
    Gorton and Andree Feghali Gorton.—Cairo: The American University in
    Cairo Press, 2017.
        p.   cm.
        ISBN: 978 977 416 842 0
        1. Jerusalem—Description and travel
        2. Archaeologists—Biography
        I.   Gorton, Andree Feghali (jt. auth.)
        II. Title
        915.694

1 2 3 4 5   21 20 19 18 17

Designed by Fatiha Bouzidi
Layout by Cherif Abdullah
Printed in the United States of America

Contents

Introduction

Oh! Jerusalem! Holy for the Christians, holy for the Muslims,
holy for the Jews, from which emanates an eternal murmur
of lamentations and prayers!" —Pierre Loti, *Le Galilée*

There is clearly "something about Jerusalem." It would be idle to speculate about why this place, which entered history in the late second millennium BC as a small agricultural settlement surrounded by hostile nomadic tribes, would become the central focus on earth for the three great monotheistic religions. This it did, of course, and the tenacity with which each has clung to these arid hills despite sieges, sacks, and wholesale banishments, invasions, massacres, and occupations, is both impressive and puzzling, no matter what belief-set one might approach it from. As a result its old stones have had to soak up more blood, witness more pain and destruction than the human mind can comprehend. This book will not dwell on that aspect—but it is there, the specter at the feast.

From the late seventeenth century to the end of the nineteenth, it seems that everyone in Europe and North America who could, did visit Jerusalem; and few resisted the temptation to record and publish their impressions for posterity. Older journeys are precious for their date, being a record of a vanished past, the Levant in Byzantine, early Islamic, or Crusader times. Many, however, are much less informative about Jerusalem than about the journey itself and the heart of the voyager.

Once in the Holy City, the pilgrims' faculties were often overwhelmed by devotion. He or she was taken in hand by touts and guides, each having exclusive authority over a stone, a cave, a pool, or a hill said to relate to Solomon's Temple, Christ's Passion, or Muhammad's Night Journey; with a few exceptions, the gullible pilgrims saw the city through the prism of scripture, punctuating their fervid descriptions with chapter and verse. All too many seem cut from the same repetitive cloth, and strong is the head that would not nod while reading yet another gushing account of treading where He trod.

How to deal—in such a small book—with a city that is both terrestrial and celestial, over which history has ridden so heavily? Of necessity patchily, partially; but hopefully without bias or an excess of "Oh! Jerusalem!"

Geography of History and Belief

Hundreds of pilgrims of diverse religions have described their experiences over the centuries. The real city was seen through the lens of faith, the surviving stones through the details of the Torah, the Gospels, or the Quran. A dose of salutary realism is provided by the formidable archaeologist Dame Kathleen

Kenyon, who literally dug up Jerusalem as well as Jericho. More recent digs at the Wall have uncovered important vestiges of Second Temple era buildings, but these would not have been known to our travelers.

Reality Check, 1867
Kathleen Kenyon

Jerusalem to-day therefore received its form in AD 135. Almost the only link with the Jerusalem of New Testament times is the great platform of the Temple built by Herod the Great. Visible links with Old Testament Jerusalem are non-existent, though a Temple platform must have dominated the city from the time of Solomon in the tenth century BC. Roman quarrying on the surface of the hill and the effects of man and nature on the slopes have removed most of the internal buildings of ancient Jerusalem.

Convenient Proximity, 1844
Alexander William Kinglake

A Protestant, familiar with the Holy Scriptures, but ignorant of the tradition and geography of modern Jerusalem, finds himself a good deal "mazed" when he first looks for the sacred sites. The Holy Sepulchre is not in a field without the walls, but in the midst, and in the best part of the town, under the roof of the great church. . . . You descend into the interior by a few steps, and there find an altar with burning tapers. This is the spot held in greater sanctity than any other in Jerusalem. When you have seen enough of it, you feel perhaps weary of the busy crowd, and inclined for a gallop; you ask your dragoman whether there will be time before sunset to send for horses and take a ride to Mount Calvary. "Mount Calvary, signor?" *eccolo!* It is *upstairs—on the first floor.* . . . The Church of the Holy Sepulchre comprises very compendiously almost all the spots associated with the closing career of Our Lord. Just there, on your right, He stood and wept— by the pillar on your left, He was scourged. . . . Even the spot where the cock crew when Peter denied his Master is ascertained and surrounded by the walls of an Armenian convent.

Antiquity/Early Middle Ages

When Jerusalem appears to the historical record, its neighborhood was already a contested and violent one. The first millennium BC saw its establishment as the capital of a predominantly Jewish kingdom, with many vicissitudes such as

the Babylonian Captivity and the Roman Conquest, which
culminated in the destruction of most of the city.

A Very Early Pilgrim, AD 332–33
The Bordeaux Pilgrim

Thence to Jerusalem: total [distance] from Caesarea to
Jerusalem twenty-six miles, four halts, four changes.
There are in Jerusalem two large pools at the side of the
temple; that is, one upon the hand, and one upon the left,
which were made by Solomon; and further in the city
are twin pools with five porticoes, which are called Beth-
saida. There persons who have been sick for many years
are cured; the pools contain water which is red when it is
disturbed. There is also here a crypt, in which Solomon
used to torture devils.

Here is also the corner of an exceeding high tower,
where our Lord ascended and the tempter said to Him, 'If
thou be the Son of God, cast thyself down from hence.' . . .

Under the pinnacle of the tower are many rooms, and
here was Solomon's palace. There also is the chamber in which
he sat and wrote the (Book of) Wisdom; this chamber is

covered with a single stone. There are also large subterranean reservoirs for water and pools constructed with great labor. And in the building itself, where stood the temple which Solomon built, they say that the blood of Zacharias which was shed upon the stone pavement before the altar remains to this day. There are also to be seen the marks of the nails in the shoes of the soldiers who slew him, throughout the whole enclosure, so plain that you would think they were impressed upon wax. There are two statues of Hadrian, and not far from the Statues there is a perforated stone, to which the Jews come every year and anoint it, bewail themselves with groans, rend their garments, and so depart.

Speaking in Tongues, c. AD 385
St. Silvia of Aquitaine

And since in that province some of the people know both Syriac and Greek, but others Greek alone or Syriac alone, and since, therefore, the bishop (although he may know Syriac) always speaks Greek, and never Syriac, a priest always stands by who interprets in Syriac what the bishop says in Greek, so that all may understand the explanations.

And since it is necessary that the lessons read in church shall be read in Greek, a man stands by who interprets in Syriac that the people may receive instruction.

And that the Latins, who know neither Syriac nor Greek, may not be saddened, an explanation is also given to them in Latin by those brothers and sisters present who understand both Greek and Latin. But above everything else it seemed to me very pleasing and admirable that the hymns, antiphons, and lessons, as well as the prayers said by the bishop, always contain expressions suitable to the day which is being observed, and the place where the service is being held . . . and these three prayers offered, behold censers are brought into the cave of the Anastasis (Resurrection), so that the whole Basilica of the Anastasis is filled with odours.

Seljuk and Fatimid Period

Jerusalem native Shams al-Din al-Muqaddasi and Iranian pilgrim Nasir-i-Khusrau offer invaluable vignettes of the city a generation before the calamitous First Crusade.

Incomparable Jerusalem, AD 972
al-Muqaddasi

The buildings of the Holy City are of stone, and you will find nowhere finer or more solid constructions. In no place will you meet with a people more chaste. Provisions are most excellent here, the markets are clean, the mosque is of the largest, and nowhere are Holy Places more numerous. The grapes are enormous, and there are no quinces to equal those of the Holy City. In Jerusalem are all manner of learned men and doctors, and for this reason the hearts of men of intelligence yearn towards her. All the year round, never are her streets empty of strangers. Now one day at Busrah I was seated in the assembly of the Chief Kadi Abu Yahya ibn Bahram, and the conversation turned on the city of Cairo. Then one said, speaking to me, "And can any city be more illustrious?" I replied, "Why, yes, my own native town!" Said he, "But is any pleasanter than Cairo?" I answered, "Yes again, my native town." It was said, "Ah, but Cairo is the more excellent, and the more beautiful, and the more productive of good things, and the more spacious." Still, to each and all I replied, "Not so! It is my native town . . . ."

"And as to Jerusalem being the pleasantest of places in the way of climate, why the cold there does not injure, and the heat is not noxious. And as to her being the finest city, why, has any seen elsewhere buildings finer, or cleaner, or a mosque that is more beautiful. And as for the Holy City being the most productive of all places in good things, why Allah—may He be exalted—has gathered together here all the fruits of the lowlands, and of the plains, and of the hill country, even all those of the most opposite kinds; such as the orange and the almond, the date and the nut, the fig and the banana, besides milk in plenty, and honey and sugar. And as to the excellence of the City! Why, is not this to be the plain of marshalling on the Day of Judgment; where the gathering together and the appointment will take place?"

Disadvantages of Jerusalem. Still, Jerusalem has some disadvantages. Thus, it is reported as found written in the Torah, that "Jerusalem is as a golden basin filled with scorpions." Then you will not find baths more filthy than those of the Holy City; nor in any town are provisions dearer. Learned men are few, and the Christians numerous, and the same are unmannerly in the public places. In the hostelries taxes are heavy on all that is sold, for there are guards at every gate, and no one is able to sell aught whereby to obtain a profit, except he be satisfied with but little gain. In this City the oppressed have no succour; the meek are molested, and the rich envied. Jurisconsults remain unvisited, and erudite men have no renown; also the schools are unattended, for there are no lectures. Everywhere the Christians and the Jews have the upper hand; and the mosque is void of either congregation or assembly of learned men.

An Iranian Pilgrim in Fatimid Times, 1017
Nasir-i-Khusrau

I now propose to make a description of the Holy City. Jerusalem is a city set on a hill, and there is no water therein, except what falls in rain. The villages round have springs of water, but the Holy City has no springs. The city is enclosed by strong walls of stone, mortared, and there are iron gates. Round about the city there are no trees, for it is all built on the rock. Jerusalem is a very great city, and, at the time of my visit, there were in it twenty thousand men. It has high, well-built, and clean bazaars. All the streets are paved with slabs of stone; and wheresoever there was a hill or a height, they have cut it down and made it level, so that as soon as the rain falls the whole place is washed clean. There are in the city numerous artificers, and each craft has a separate bazaar. . . .

The Friday Mosque (which is the Aksa) lies on the east side of the city, and (as before noticed) one of the walls of the mosque (area) is on the Wadi Jahannum. When you examine this wall, which is on the Wadi, from the outside of the mosque, you may see that for the space of a hundred cubits it is built up of huge stones, set without mortar or cement. Inside the mosque (area) it is level all along the summit of this wall. The [Aksa] mosque occupies the position it does because of the stone of the Sakhrah. This stone of the Sakhrah is that which God—be He exalted and glorified!—commanded Moses to institute as the Kiblah (or direction to be faced at prayer). After this command had come down, and Moses had instituted it as the Kiblah, he himself lived but a brief time, for of a sudden was his life cut short. Then came the days of Solomon—upon him be peace!—who, seeing that the rock (of the Sakhrah) was the Kiblah point, built a mosque round about the rock, whereby the rock stood in the midst of the mosque, which became the oratory of the people.

So it remained down to the days of our Prophet Muhammad, the Chosen One—upon him be blessings and peace!—who likewise at first recognised this to be the Kiblah, turning towards it at his prayers; but God— be He exalted and glorified!—afterwards commanded him to institute, as the Kiblah, the House of the Ka'abah [at Mekkah]. . . . Adjacent to the east wall, and when you have reached the south [eastern] angle [of the Haram Area]—the Kiblah point lying before you, south, but somewhat aside—there is an underground mosque, to which you descend by many steps. It is situated immediately to the north of the [south] wall of the Haram Area, covering a space measuring twenty ells by fifteen, and it has a roof of stone, supported on marble columns. Here was the Cradle of Jesus. The cradle is of stone, and large enough for a man to make therein his prayer prostrations. I myself said my prayers there.

The cradle is fixed into the ground, so that it cannot be moved. This cradle is where Jesus was laid during his childhood, and where He held converse with the people. The cradle itself, in this mosque, has been made the Mihrab [or oratory]; and there is likewise, on the east side of this mosque, the Mihrab Maryam [or Oratory of Mary]; and another Mihrab, which is that of Zakariyyi [Zachariah]—peace be upon him! Above these Mihrabs are written the verses revealed in the Kuran that relate respectively to Zachariah and to Mary. They say that Jesus—peace be upon Him!—was born in the place where this mosque stands. On the shaft of one of the columns there is impressed a mark as though a person had gripped the stone with two fingers; and they say that Mary, when taken in the pangs of labour, did thus with one hand seize upon the stone. This mosque is known by the title of Mahd Isa [the Cradle of Jesus]—peace be upon Him!—and they have suspended a great number of lamps there, of silver and of brass, that are lighted every night.

Crusader Times

The sack of Jerusalem by the frenzied warriors of the First Crusade, who put to the sword nearly the entire population of the city regardless of age, sex, or religion still haunts relations between the communities throughout the Levant. The Abbot Daniel, who was probably attached to the Monastery of Suriev, made his pilgrimage only a few years after the

Crusader conquest of the city in 1099. Rabbi Benjamin of Tudela in Moorish Spain traveled extensively through the Mediterranean countries, his attention often focused on the size and state of the Jewish communities in each place.

Deeds of the Franks, 1100–1101
Anonymous chronicle

The memoir Gesta Francorum et aliorum Hierosylymytanorum *("Deeds of the Franks and Other Jerusalemites") of this nameless eyewitness was used by many later chroniclers.*

One of our knights, named Lethold, clambered up the wall of the city, and no sooner had he ascended than the defenders fled from the walls and through the city. Our men followed, killing and slaying even to the Temple of Solomon, where the slaughter was so great that our men waded in blood up to their ankles. . . .

Count Raymond brought his army and his tower up near the wall from the south, but between the tower and the wall there was a very deep ditch. Then our men took counsel how they might fill it, and had it proclaimed by heralds that anyone who carried three stones to the ditch would receive one denarius. The work of filling it required three days and three nights, and when at length the ditch was filled, they moved the tower up to the wall, but the men defending this portion of the wall fought desperately with stones and fire. When the Count heard that the Franks were already in the city, he said to his men, "Why do you loiter? Lo, the Franks are even now within the city."

The Emir who commanded the Tower of St. David surrendered to the Count and opened that gate at which the pilgrims had always been accustomed to pay tribute. But this time the pilgrims entered the city, pursuing and killing the Saracens up to the Temple of Solomon, where the enemy gathered in force. The battle raged throughout the day, so that the Temple was covered with their blood. When the pagans had been overcome, our men seized great numbers, both men and women, either killing them or keeping them captive, as they wished. On the roof of the Temple a great number of pagans of both sexes had assembled, and these were taken under the protection of Tancred and Gaston of Beert. Afterward, the army scattered throughout the city and took possession of the gold and silver, the horses and mules, and the houses filled with goods of all kinds.

Rejoicing and weeping for joy, our people came to the Sepulchre of Jesus our Saviour to worship and pay their debt [i.e., fulfill crusading vows by worshiping at the Sepulcher]. At dawn our men cautiously went up to the roof of the Temple and attacked Saracen men and women, beheading them with naked swords. Some of the Saracens, however, leaped from the Temple roof. Tancred, seeing this, was greatly angered.

A Russian Abbot in Crusader Jerusalem, c. 1107
Abbot Daniel (Danilo)

The following is a description of the Holy Light, which descends upon the Holy Sepulchre, as the Lord vouchsafed to show it to me, His wicked and unworthy servant. . . . I will only describe it in perfect truth as I have seen it. On Holy Friday, after Vespers, they clean the Holy Sepulchre and wash all the lamps that are there; they fill the lamps with pure oil without water and after having put in the wicks, leave them unlighted. They affix the seals to the Tomb at the second hour of the night. At the same time they extinguish all the lamps and wax candles in every church in Jerusalem.

On the morrow, Holy Saturday, at the sixth hour of the day, everyone assembles in front of the Church of the Holy Resurrection; foreigners and natives people from all countries, from Babylon, from Egypt, and from every part of the world, come together on that day in countless numbers; the crowd fills the open space round the church and round the place of the Crucifixion. The crush is terrible, and the turmoil so great that many persons are suffocated in the dense crowd of people who stand, unlighted tapers in hand, waiting for the opening of the church doors. The priests alone are inside the church, and priests and crowd alike wait for the arrival of the Prince and his suite; then, the doors being opened, the people rush in, pushing and jostling each other, and fill the church and the galleries, for the church alone could not contain such a multitude.

A large portion of the crowd has to remain outside round Golgotha and the place of the skull, and as far as the spot where the crosses were set up; every place is filled with an innumerable multitude. All the people, within and without the church, cry ceaselessly, "Kyrie Eleison" (Lord, have mercy upon us); and this cry is so loud that the whole building resounds and vibrates with it. The faithful shed torrents of tears; even he who has a heart of stone cannot refrain from weeping; each one, searching the innermost depths of his soul, thinks of his sins, and says secretly to himself, "Will my sins prevent the descent of the Holy Light?" The faithful remain thus weeping with heavy heart; Prince Baldwin himself looks contrite and greatly humbled; torrents of tears stream from his eyes; and his suite stand pensively around him near the high altar, opposite the Tomb.

Saturday, about the seventh hour, Prince Baldwin, with his suite, left his house, and, proceeding on foot towards the Sepulchre of our Lord, sent to the hospice of St. Sabbas for the abbot and monks of St. Sabbas; the abbot, followed by the monks, thereupon set out for the Holy Sepulchre, and I, unworthy, went with them. When we reached the Prince we all saluted him; he returned our salute and directed the abbot and me, the lowly one, to walk by his side, whilst the other abbots and the monks went in front, and the suite followed behind. . . . The Prince ordered the Abbot of St. Sabbas to take up a position over beyond the Tomb, with his monks and the orthodox priests; as for me, the lowly one, he directed me to place myself higher up, above the doors of the Holy Sepulchre, in front of the high altar, so that I could see through the doors of the Tomb; these doors, three in number, were sealed up with the royal seal. The Latin priests stood by the high altar. . . .

At the end of the ninth hour, when they commenced chanting the Canticle of the passage (of the Red Sea), "*Cantabo Domino*," a small cloud, coming suddenly from the east, rested above the open dome of the church; fine rain fell on the Holy Sepulchre, and wet us and all those who were around the Tomb. It was at this moment that the Holy Light suddenly illuminated the Holy Sepulchre, shining with an awe-aspiring and splendid brightness. The bishop, who was followed by four deacons, then opened the doors of the Tomb, and entered with the taper of Prince Baldwin so as to light it first at the Holy Light; he afterwards returned it to the Prince, who resumed his place, holding, with great joy, the taper in his hands. We lighted our tapers from that of the Prince, and so passed on the flame to everyone in the church. . . . .

The morning of Holy Sunday, after having chanted the matins, exchanged kisses with the abbot and monks, and received absolution, we started about the first hour of the day for the Holy Sepulchre: the abbot cross in hand, and all the monks singing the hymn, "Immortal One, Thou hast deigned to go down into the Tomb." Having entered the Holy Sepulchre, we covered the life-giving tomb of the Lord with kisses and scorching tears; we breathed with ecstasy the perfume which the presence of the Holy Ghost had left; and we gazed in admiration on the lamps which still burned with a bright and marvellous splendor.

Jerusalem in 1187, 1187
Rabbi Benjamin of Tudela

Jerusalem . . . is a small city, fortified by three walls. It is full of people whom the Mohammedans call Jacobites, Syrians, Greeks, Georgians and Franks, and people of all tongues. It contains a dyeing-house, for which the Jews pay a small rent annually to the king, on condition that besides the Jews no other dyers be allowed in Jerusalem. There are about 200 Jews who dwell under the Tower of David in one corner of the city. The lower portion of the wall of the Tower of David, to the extent of about ten cubits, is part of the ancient foundation set up by our ancestors, the remaining portion having been built by the Mohammedans. There is no structure in the whole city stronger than the Tower of David. The city also contains two buildings, from one of which—the hospital—there issue forth four hundred knights; and therein all the sick who come thither are lodged and cared for in life and in death.

The other building is called the Temple of Solomon; it is the palace built by Solomon the king of Israel. Three hundred knights are quartered there, and issue therefrom every day for military exercise, besides those who come from the land of the Franks and the other parts of Christendom, having taken upon themselves to serve there a year or two until their vow is fulfilled. In Jerusalem is the great church called the Sepulchre, and here is the burial-place of Jesus, unto which the Christians make pilgrimages. Jerusalem has four gates—the gate of Abraham, the gate of David, the gate of Zion, and the gate of Gushpat, which is the gate of Jehoshaphat, facing our ancient Temple, now called *Templum Domini*.

Upon the site of the sanctuary Omar ben al Khataab erected an edifice with a very large and magnificent cupola, into which the Gentiles do not bring any image or effigy, but they merely come there to pray. In front of this place is the western wall, which is one of the walls of the Holy of Holies. This is called the Gate of Mercy, and thither come all the Jews to pray before the wall of the court of the Temple. In Jerusalem, attached to the palace which belonged to Solomon, are the stables built by him, forming a very substantial structure, composed of large stones, and the like of it is not to be seen anywhere in the world. There is also visible up to this day the pool used by the priests before offering their sacrifices, and the Jews coming thither write their names upon the wall. The gate of Jehoshaphat leads to the valley of Jehoshaphat, which is the gathering-place of nations.

Here is the pillar called Absalom's Hand, and the sepulchre of King Uzziah. In the neighbourhood is also a great spring, called the Waters of Siloam, connected with the brook of Kidron. Over the spring is a large structure dating from the time of our ancestors, but little water is found, and the people of Jerusalem for the most part drink the rain-water, which they collect in cisterns in their houses. . . .

In front of Jerusalem is Mount Zion, on which there is no building, except a place of worship belonging to the Christians. Facing Jerusalem for a distance of three miles are the cemeteries belonging to the Israelites, who in the days of old buried their dead in caves, and upon each sepulchre is a dated inscription, but the Christians destroy the sepulchres, employing the stones thereof in building their houses. These sepulchres reach as far as Zelzah in the territory of Benjamin. Around Jerusalem are high mountains.

Mamluk and Ottoman Era Travelers

Ah, one's first sight of the Holy City! Intense expectations often led to something of a letdown, though for a few travelers the enthusiasm of the idea of Jerusalem survived, for a while at least, contact with a living, dusty, intensely mercantile city.

First Impressions of Jerusalem, 1848
Harriet Martineau

We considered ourselves most fortunate in our lodgement at Jerusalem—I mean in the position of our rooms at Salvador's hotel. The house would not contain the whole of our party, and three went to lodgings. But we ladies had light airy rooms opening upon the highest platform of the hotel—this platform being the roof of a lower set of chambers. I was never tired of gazing abroad from the parapet of our little terrace, from which I could command a large extent of the flat roofs of the city, and of its picturesque walls. The narrow, winding street far below, which we overlooked almost from end to end, was the Via Dolorosa; and it was spanned midway by the Ecce Homo arch.

This Mournful Way, where I rarely saw any one walking, attracted the eye all the more from its being almost the only street we had a glimpse of; the streets of Eastern cities being so narrow as not to be visible from a height. Some few were traceable by a comparison of the lines of house tops, and the guidance of the minarets which sprang from among the roofs, tall and light as the poplar from the long grass of the meadow: but the only street which we could look down into was the Via Dolorosa. Beyond the city, and directly opposite, rote the long slope of Olivet.

It was now the time of full moon; and evening after evening, I leaned on that parapet, watching for the coming up of the large yellow orb behind the ridge of the Mount of Olives. By day the slopes of the Mount were green with the springing wheat, and dappled with the shade of the olive clumps. By night, those clumps and lines of trees were dark amidst the lights and shadows cast by the moon; and they guided the eye, in the absence of daylight, to the most interesting points—the descent to the brook Kedron, the road to Bethany, and the place whence Jesus is said to have looked over upon the noble city when he pronounced its doom. . . .

A lady stood in a solemn attitude, with folded arms and bowed head, while we examined the Calvary. When we moved on, she threw back her veil, and we recognized her as an English lady, now a Russian Countess, whom we met daily at the *table d'hôte* at Cairo. With a most extraordinary gesture, she cast aside her veil, threw open her arms, prostrated herself at the altar, and not only covered the place of the cross with kiss, but laid her head into the socket. I could look no longer, and hastened away to see the one truly interesting thing in the church. The tombs of Godfrey of Bouillon and his brother Baldwin were once shown here—sarcophagi on small marble pillars. It is said that the Greeks destroyed them; and we could find only the place where these heroes were said to have been buried. Two stone seats were called the tombs; but we understood them as merely pointing out the locality. . . . His sword and spurs were here; relics, of whose genuineness there is no reason to doubt. When I handled them, I was glad I had come. The sword is not very heavy, plain, with a hilt which seemed to us to suit rather a small hand.

In the area in front of the church, there is always a little market of beads, crucifixes, carved shells, etc.; and here the beggars collect, alarming the stranger into giving alms, under penalty of contact with their clothes. The dragoman had to lay about him with a stout stick before we had any peace.

First Glimpse, 1895
Pierre Loti

The day of our arrival in Jerusalem—a day we have dreamt of in advance, like the pilgrims of old, during their forty days in the desert. . . . In the distance, a large city begins to appear, perched on melancholy, stony mountains. A collection of scattered buildings: convents, churches of all styles and origins. Seen through the driving rain or dust, it looks vague and confusing, disappearing from time to time as big rolling clouds hide it from our view.

To the left of the mountains, nothing more than disappointing, ordinary structures; but up on the right, there is Jerusalem the antique, looking like the pictures in rustic missals: Jerusalem, recognizable among all cities, with its fierce walls, the stone roofs of its cupolas; Jerusalem brooding and lofty, enclosed behind its ramparts, all under a black sky. . . .

Crossing a deep trench, we begin to climb up a street through the clutch of pitiful constructions blanketing the left-hand hill—hotels, train stations, factories—and the somber crenellated walls rising up to the right. People of all nations crowd around: Arabs, Turks, Bedouins, but especially unexpected Northern personages: long blond beards emerging from fur caps, Russian pilgrims, poor ragged moujiks. And finally, we climb up into the city with its high walls towering over us, its ramparts, its strangely gloomy mass, up we climb through this crowd on a road made glorious by sieges and battles, where so many Crusaders fell on account of their faith. . . . It took a few moments to understand where we were, and then came a wave of emotion, but all in a furtive, disturbing

jumble carried along by the noise, the wind, and the proximity of locomotives and tourist agencies. . . . Finally, reaching the top, we pass under the great arched gate of Jerusalem, completely free of any concern save to get out of the rain and take refuge in some inn, the rain which is now falling in fast, icy torrents.

Disappointed Expectations, 1849–50
Gustave Flaubert

A sleepless night, what with the mosquitos, the horses, and the idea that I will see Jerusalem in the morning . . . .

At every instant I expect to see Jerusalem—but don't. The road (the barely distinguishable vestige of an ancient path) is execrable, no way to trot the horses. The occasional dry-stone enclosure in this landscape of stones. Finally, in the corner of a wall, in a courtyard with olive trees, I spy a Muslim holy man all alone. A little further along a few Arabs who shout "al-Quds! al-Quds!" (seems to me they pronounce "*codess*"). Twenty-seven women all wearing blue blouses, on their way back from the bazaar; and three minutes later, *Jerusalem*. So clean, with all its walls still standing. I imagined Jesus going in and out on his way up to the Mount of Olives.

Through the gate ahead, I can see the mountains of Hebron behind the city, on my right, all transparent and vaporous. All else is dry, hard, and grey; the raw whiteness of the light gives it a wintry look, despite the warm hues, quite puzzling . . . .

It's already our third day in Jerusalem. I have experienced none of the emotions I expected before coming: no religious enthusiasm, no flights of imagination, no hatred for priests (which would at least be *something*). Standing before everything I look at, I feel more hollow than an empty barrel. This morning, at the Holy Sepulchre, a dog would undeniably have been more moved than I was. Whose fault, merciful God? Theirs? Yours? Mine? Theirs, I think; then mine, but especially *yours*. How false it all is, what lies they tell, how sloppy it all is, tarted up, varnished and packaged into merchandise, propaganda and commerce. Jerusalem is a slaughterhouse within walls.

A Flat and Unimposing View, 1850
William Bartlett

Nothing can be more flat and unimposing than the first view of Jerusalem by the Jaffa road. We passed across a high bleak tract of country, the surface of which is everywhere so rocky and uneven, that the horse stumbles at every step. The hills are totally without character, and the general scene tame, wearisome, and depressing. Here and there, indeed, the rugged slopes are thinly veiled by terraces of grey olives, or a poor looking field of corn seems struggling for life in the arid plain; but the general aspect is sterility itself . . . . As we draw nearer, however, the view becomes somewhat more imposing. The Valley of Hinnom slopes down on the right, gradually sinking till it forms a deep and rugged glen beneath Mount Zion, the walls and towers of which stand out in striking relief.

The towers of the citadel have also an imposing effect, increased by its bold outwork and profound fosse; while the Jaffa or Bethlehem gate, of handsome Saracenic architecture, forms an admirable centre to the picture . . . . These battlemented bulwarks, flanked with towers, perforated with openings for arrows, and overlapped by a lofty minaret, have a strikingly picturesque effect. Moreover, as this is the principal entrance to the city, it presents, in the morning and evening, a very animated spectacle. Women, bearing baskets of grapes, figs, or pigeons from the neighbouring villages; peasants, driving before them asses laden with vegetables; Bedouins, conducting files of camels, bearing masses of stone for new buildings, continue to pour along in a continuous stream. Monks slowly amble in upon their asses from some of the neighbouring convents, or European residents dash past from their country houses or summer encampments in the neighbourhood. Large flocks of black-haired goats, from which the city is supplied with milk, ascend from the Valley of Ilinnom. And at this hour there is a show of life and animation which might seem to indicate an important and flourishing city.

Dreary City, 1898
Edouard Schuré

In the dreary city, nary a passing carriage, not a single stroller to be seen, only bells, calling to each other in the air. The streets are as narrow as bottomless gutters; no flowers, no gardens. Here and there a solitary cypress in a bare strip of earth, in front of deserted arcades. Nearly windowless houses huddle together: terrorized by plagues of the past, or hoping for future glory? The balustraded terraces are topped with small cupolas, white bosses that—seen from above—give the whole city the air of a Muslim cemetery; but one's gaze is drawn to two enormous black domes which dominate all the others. One rises in the centre of the city: that's the Holy Sepulchre, the tomb of Christ. The other, where once stood the Temple of Solomon, is the Mosque of Omar or the Tomb of Jehovah. The dwellings of the living disappear, overwhelmed by the tombs of the gods. . . .

Austere and silent city! One loses oneself in the labyrinth of narrow streets, meandering uphill and downhill, between lofty houses with holes, slits or dormer windows with iron bars for windows. Reused Roman stones nestle with Christian and Muslim ones in the walls; frequent demolition, constant rebuilding in the same turret and fortress style. Everywhere, alleys snaking under buildings; here, a Herodian arch spans the street; there, an expanse of Saracen wall straddles it and glares at you threateningly through murder-holes. . . . One wanders past church porticoes, a glimpse of monks praying by candlelight; losing oneself in the long tunnels, bazaars and markets, where faint lamps glow amidst the dark stalls, where Bedouins and camels jostle each other, hardly seeing each other as they push their way through this immense intestine.

The Grand Tour to the Holy Land

The Grand Tour: more (or perhaps less) than a pilgrimage. A journey to be enjoyed for some, endured for others, more or less arduous in inverse proportion to one's (or one's parents') means. Piety took a back seat to being seen during, and being heard or read afterward.

Returning from an Excursion, 1789
Buck Whaley

On returning to the City by the Valley of Jehoshaphat, you are shown the ruins of the palace where Solomon kept his concubines; and which you are taught to believe was once surrounded by extensive gardens, displaying all the beauties of exquisite taste and luxuriant fertility: but at present, this place, as well as the whole country round Jerusalem, exhibits nothing but sterility and indigence. On entering the City we examined a castle where the Turks regularly mount guard; and which, on account of its antiquity (being erected by King David), is well worth seeing. It is almost the only building that has escaped the ravages of the successive wars that have taken place. It was from a window in this castle, that King David first saw [the] fair Bathsheba, as she was bathing in a fountain, which is overlooked by the tower.

There is a terrace on the top with embrazures; but it has only a few dismounted and useless guns which have remained here since the time of the Crusades. In an apartment at the top of the castle we saw a great number of coats of mail, helmets, breast- and shoulder-plates, old spears and some shields, brought hither by Richard Coeur de Lion, at the time he undertook to take the City from the Saracens, and reduce it under the power of the Christians. . . .

Night coming on we returned to the Convent, where our friend the Governor always had a good bowl of punch *a l'Angloise* ready for us.

A Visit to the Governor, 1832–33
Alphonse de Lamartine

We were introduced into the divan, a grand saloon, without any other ornament than some carpets spread out upon the mats, with some pipes and coffee cups on the ground. The governor, surrounded by a great number of slaves, of armed Arabs and some secretaries on their knees, writing on their hands, was occupied in administering justice, and despatching his orders. He rose at our approach, and advanced to meet us. He ordered the carpets of the divan, which were likely to communicate the plague, to be removed, and substituted Egyptian mats for them, which are known to be anti-contagious.

We seated ourselves, and pipes and coffee were handed to us. My dragoman paid him in my name the customary compliments, and I thanked him myself for the care and precautions, which he so willingly and handsomely adopted in order to enable us, strangers as we were, to visit without danger the places rendered holy by our religion.

He answered with an obliging smile that he had performed no more than his duty; that the friends of Ibrahim were his friends, and that he was answerable for every hair of their heads; that he was ready and willing, not only to do for me, what he had already done, but that if I desired it, he would put himself at the head of his troops, and accompany me to every place, whither my curiosity or my religion might inspire me with the desire to go, if it was within the limits of his government, and such was the order which had been transmitted to him from the pacha.

On the other hand, he requested some information from us respecting the [Crimean] war, and particularly relative to the part which the European powers took in

the success of Ibrahim. I answered him in a manner suf-
ficient to satisfy his secret wishes, and in some measure
to flatter his own pride. I replied that Europe admired
in Ibrahim a civilizing conqueror and that in that relation, Europe took a great interest in his victories; that it
was time the East participated in the benefits of a more
enlightened administration. . . .These sentiments pen-
etrated to the heart of the old rebel of Naplous; his looks
appeared as it were to drink my very words, whilst his son
and his friends inclined their heads over mine, in order
that they might not lose a single word of this conversation, which to them was the augury of a long and peace-
able government in Samaria.

A Grand Tour Day in Jerusalem, 1860
Lady Catherine Tobin

We *wallowed* to our hotel through the dirty streets, and
filthy ill supplied bazaars—the latter entirely covered
overhead with awnings—passing many a dish of hot
kebab (small strips of meat toasted with onions on a
skewer) prepared for the evening meal. Just before dinner

we received a visit from the English Consul and Mrs. Finn—both profuse in friendly offers of service. . . .

Friday, February 3rd. In spite of threatening clouds, we set off immediately after breakfast to "do" a round of sight seeing within the city walls. Monkish tradition pretends to point out the site of every important event connected with the scriptural history of Jerusalem; nay, the remains of *buildings* are confidently asserted to be actual relics of our blessed Saviour's time!

Proceeding along the Via Dolorosa, we saw Pontius Pilate's Hall of Justice—House of Santa Veronica—House of Dives (now used as a military hospital); and a large stone, hollowed in its centre, the receptacle for *crumbs thrown from the rich man's table*!—Place from whence Pilate pronounced the "*Ecce Homo*"—Governor's Palace of that day—and House of Herod! Beneath the great altar of the Church of the "Flagellation" was discovered—say the Franciscan monks to whom it belongs— "the very pillar to which Jesus Christ was bound!" We remembered having seen half of this column some years ago at Rome.

A group of clay figures in a glass case at the back of the altar represents the flagellation of our Lord, and below the slab five silver lamps burn day and night. The church contains a few good paintings, particularly a *Madonna Dolorosa*; and there is a print of Carlo Dolci's *Madonna*, from the original picture in the Pitti Palace at Florence. We next came to the House of Simon the Pharisee, "Where are ruins of a chapel erected by the Empress Helena;" and also a manufacture of common pottery: we purchased six little earthenware lamps for half a piastre—not quite one penny farthing! Tomaso called our attention to *the* stone whereon Mary Magdalene "washed Jesus' feet with her tears, and did wipe them with the hairs of her head, &c."

From thence to Herod's Gate, near which the Crusaders entered Jerusalem under Godfrey de Bouillon, AD 1099.— House of Pontius Pilate—Two of the nine gates leading to the Mosque of Omar—Tower of Antoninus—House of Joachim and Anna, parents of the Virgin Mary; the Turks took forcible possession of this edifice, and built a mosque over it. A fountain and oblong cistern, still in use, is called the Virgin's Bath! We were now close to St. Stephen's Gate, near the spot where Stephen suffered martyrdom; and turning to the right, stood by the Pool of Bethesda—then dry; but which was formerly supplied from the Pools of Solomon, and even yet occasionally contains a little water after heavy rains. The walls are most picturesquely covered with wild flowers and creeping plants. . . .

We were told that a splendid prospect might be obtained from the Barracks; however, to our disappointment, the guard refused to admit us—as contrary to rule. Fortunately, the Turkish General in command chanced to appear at that moment, and asked our guide whether we were "English or Americans?" Tomaso replied "English travellers" whereupon the General immediately said that our request should be granted.

Jumping Cats and Chicken Coops, 1869
Mark Twain

We climbed up another hill and each pilgrim and each sinner threw his hat into the air, yelling "Jerusalem!" Perched on the eternal hills, white, sprinkled with domes and tightly enclosed in its high grey stone walls, the venerable city shone under the sun, so small!

A fast walker could go outside the walls of Jerusalem and walk entirely around the city in an hour. I do not know how else to make one understand how small it is. The appearance of the city is peculiar. It is as knobby with countless little domes as a prison door is with bolt-heads.

Every house has from one to half a dozen of these white plastered domes of stone, broad and low, sitting in the centre of, or in a cluster upon, the flat roof. Wherefore, when one looks down from an eminence, upon the compact mass of houses (so closely crowded together, in fact, that there is no appearance of streets at all, and so the city looks solid) he sees the knobbiest town in the world, except Constantinople. It looks as if it might be roofed, from centre to circumference, with inverted saucers. The monotony of the view is interrupted only by the great Mosque of Omar, the Tower of Hippicus, and one or two other buildings that rise into commanding prominence.

The houses are generally two stories high, built strongly of masonry, whitewashed or plastered outside, and have a cage of wooden lattice-work projecting in front of every window. To reproduce a Jerusalem street, it would only be necessary to up-end a chicken-coop and hang it before each window in an alley of American houses.

The streets are roughly and badly paved with stone, and are tolerably crooked—enough so to make each street appear to close together constantly and come to an end about a hundred yards ahead of a pilgrim as long as he chooses to walk in it. Projecting from the top of the lower story of many of the houses is a very narrow porch-roof or shed, without supports from below; and I have several times seen cats jump across the street from one shed to the other when they were out calling. The cats could have jumped double the distance without extraordinary exertion. I mention these things to give an idea of how narrow the streets are. Since a cat can jump across them without the least inconvenience, it is hardly necessary to state that such streets are too narrow for carriages. These vehicles cannot navigate the Holy City.

The Grand Tour Ends in Tourism, 1914
Estelle Blyth

Towards the end of our time in Palestine, tourist agencies were bringing enormous parties of tourists from America. One such party numbered five thousand persons, some of whom had to be sent through the country to Haifa while the rest "did" Jerusalem, there being no accommodation for such numbers at once. Such large unwieldy parties were a great mistake. For one thing, the programme offered attracted mainly the globe-trotting American, and not the pilgrim; and for another, Jerusalem was not capable of housing or feeding comfortably such numbers of strangers at one time.

Generally about three days were allotted to seeing Jerusalem, Jericho, Bethlehem, and Hebron, but not all gave even as long as three days; and then the unhappy people would be collected from the hotels, boarding-houses, and convents in which they had been bestowed, and rushed through the country to Haifa, the port of Galilee, while the rest of the party, left at Haifa, arrived to "do" Jerusalem. It was three lost, unhappy, and utterly exhausted ladies belonging to one of these parties who were discovered seated in our garden by my Mother. They had seen the shady paths from the church through an open door, and had wandered in, thankful to sit down for a while. They said, "We don't know where we are, and we don't know what we've seen, and we can't imagine why we ever came at all!"

Disappointed Tourists, 1922
Sir Ronald Storrs

During my first few weeks in Palestine nothing impressed me more than the variety of other people's impressions. Apart from intellectuals, who considered that Jerusalem had delivered its message to humanity (and so more or less shot its bolt) and travellers who had actually been there before, I discovered many grades of religious and geographical ignorance. Some of my correspondents "had not heard there was such a place. Others "had always thought it was a place in the Bible."

I was occasionally asked whether the Church of the Holy Sepulchre was AD or BC. A baronet begged me to show him the way to the Villa Rose, which he had been told he really ought to see before leaving. It proved to be his "approach" to the Via Dolorosa. Most visitors fell into one of two categories, the ecstatic who prostrated themselves at every site, even when two or more were credited with the same event, and the sceptical who explained away evidence and tradition which they would have accepted implicitly for Tiberius or Shakespeare, and who seemed to expect a macadamized Gethsemane and a Temple of Solomon rendered in corrugated iron. Many were "disappointed with Jerusalem" because "it was so different to what they had expected." The roads were even worse than the hotels and in place of the Holy City they found a smell.

Jewish Jerusalem

Flavius Josephus provides a retrospective eyewitness description of Second Temple Jerusalem. After the wholesale destruction of the city in AD 70, there were not many Jewish monuments for visitors to describe, though many mentioned the Wailing Wall and Jewish Quarter. One of the saddest and

most disturbing impressions left by the memoirs of pilgrims and Grand Tour voyagers alike is the contemptuous and scornful language many of them reserved for the Jewish inhabitants of the city and their Quarter, betraying an ugly bias that does the writers no credit.

The Second Temple, AD 93–95
Flavius Josephus

When you go through these [first] cloisters, unto the second [court of the] temple, there was a partition made of stone all round, whose height was three cubits: its construction was very elegant; upon it stood pillars, at equal distances from one another, declaring the law of purity, some in Greek, and some in Roman letters, that "no foreigner should go within that sanctuary" for that second [court of the] temple was called "the Sanctuary," and was ascended to by fourteen steps from the first court. This court was four-square, and had a wall about it peculiar to itself; the height of its buildings, although it were on the outside forty cubits, was hidden by the steps, and on the inside that height was but twenty-five cubits; for it being built over against a higher part of the hill with steps, it was no further to be entirely discerned within, being covered by the hill itself.

Beyond these thirteen steps there was the distance of ten cubits; this was all plain; whence there were other steps, each of five cubits a-piece, that led to the gates, which gates on the north and south sides were eight, on each of those sides four, and of necessity two on the east. For since there was a partition built for the women on that side, as the proper place wherein they were to worship, there was a necessity for a second gate for them: this gate was cut out of its wall, over against the first gate.

There was also on the other sides one southern and one northern gate, through which was a passage into the court of the women; for as to the other gates, the women were not allowed to pass through them; nor when they went through their own gate could they go beyond their own wall. This place was allotted to the women of our own country, and of other countries, provided they were of the same nation, and that equally. The western part of this court had no gate at all, but the wall was built entire on that side. But then the cloisters which were betwixt the gates extended from the wall inward, before the chambers; for they were supported by very fine and large pillars. These cloisters were single, and, excepting their magnitude, were no way inferior to those of the lower court. . . .

As to the holy house itself, which was placed in the midst [of the inmost court], that most sacred part of the temple, it was ascended to by twelve steps; and in front its height and its breadth were equal, and each a hundred cubits, though it was behind forty cubits narrower; for on its front it had what may be styled shoulders on each side, that passed twenty cubits further. Its first gate was seventy cubits high, and twenty-five cubits broad; but this gate had no doors; for it represented the universal visibility of heaven, and that it cannot be excluded from any place. Its front was covered with gold all over, and through it the first part of the house, that was more inward, did all of it appear; which, as it was very large, so did all the parts about the more inward gate appear to shine to those that saw them; but then, as the entire house was divided into two parts within, it was only the first part of it that was open to our view.

Its height extended all along to ninety cubits in height . . . , and its length was fifty cubits, and its breadth twenty. But that gate which was at this end of the first part of the house was, as we have already observed, all over covered with gold, as was its whole wall about it; it had also golden vines above it, from which clusters of grapes hung as tall as a man's height. But then this house, as it was divided into two parts, the inner part was lower than the appearance of the outer, and had golden doors of fifty-five cubits altitude, and sixteen in breadth; but before these doors there was a veil of equal largeness with the doors. It was a Babylonian curtain, embroidered with blue, and fine linen, and scarlet, and purple, and of a contexture that was truly wonderful. Nor was this mixture of colors without its mystical interpretation, but was a kind of image of the universe; for by the scarlet there seemed to be enigmatically signified fire, by the fine flax the earth, by the blue the air, and by the purple the sea; two of them having their colors the foundation of this resemblance;

but the fine flax and the purple have their own origin for that foundation, the earth producing the one, and the sea the other. This curtain had also embroidered upon it all that was mystical in the heavens, excepting that of the [twelve] signs, representing living creatures. . . .

Now the outward face of the temple . . . was covered all over with plates of gold of great weight, and, at the first rising of the sun, reflected back a very fiery splendor, and made those who forced themselves to look upon it to turn their eyes away, just as they would have done at the sun's own rays. But this temple appeared to strangers, when they were coming to it at a distance, like a mountain covered with snow; for as to those parts of it that were not gilt, they were exceeding white. On its top it had spikes with sharp points, to prevent any pollution of it by birds sitting upon it. Of its stones, some of them were forty-five cubits in length, five in height, and six in breadth. Before this temple stood the altar, fifteen cubits high, and equal both in length and breadth; each of which dimensions was fifty cubits. The figure it was built in was a square, and it had corners like horns; and the passage up to it was

by an insensible acclivity. It was formed without any iron tool, nor did any such iron tool so much as touch it at any time. There was also a wall of partition, about a cubit in height, made of fine stones, and so as to be grateful to the sight; this encompassed the holy house and the altar, and kept the people that were on the outside off from the priests.

The Wailing Wall, 1872

Amy Fullerton

This morning I took my guide Ibrahim, and went to the Stones of Wailing. We passed through the Jewish bazaar, and many curious nooks and corners of this singular city, containing generations upon generations who have raised fresh buildings upon the crumbling dust of ages, and left many streets and thoroughfares almost buried and tunnelled under the mounds. Overlapping houses, overarched streets, the narrowest possible paths, leading through the bazaars, with their counters almost touching each other, the constant traffic, the crowd of varied costumes—all combine to form a picture which no imagination could have devised. We at last turned into a comparatively wider approach, and before us rose a wall of enormous height. It formed one side of a narrow alley. The stones of this area-wall of the Temple—for such it was—were of the most massive appearance, many of them bevelled, as all the ancient Jewish, and to go even farther back, as was also the Jebusite stone-work.

Kneeling, standing, and sitting in groups, were the Jews; some listening to their rabbi reading the Law and books of Moses; some gazing in an abstracted manner at the groups of English who began to assemble; some, in paroxysms of weeping, were thrusting their heads into the very crevices of the stones, as if calling upon them to bear witness to their lamentations and strivings, that they should be alone beholden of their despair. These paid not the slightest attention to the buzz of the multitude, nor to the chattering of a group of young Jewish women who had gathered round a Californian traveller seated on the ground with his back against the opposite wall, and making notes of the scene with great *sang-froid*.

Christian Monuments

Every Christian visitor described his or her visit to the Church of the Holy Sepulcher; Arculfus provides a rare account of Jerusalem's preeminent church, originally built by Constantine in the fouth century, sacked by the Sassanid Persians in AD 614, rebuilt by the Byzantine Emperor Heraclius in 630.

Much of the early church described by Arculfus was destroyed in AD 1009 on the orders of the Fatimid Caliph al-Hakim bi-Amrillah.

An Early Description, c. AD 670
Arculfus

And certainly this very great Church, the whole of which is of stone, was formed of marvellous roundness in every part, rising up from the foundations in three walls, which have one roof at a lofty elevation, having a broad pathway between each wall and the next; there are also three altars in three dexterously formed places of the middle wall. This round and very large church, with the above-mentioned altars, looking one to the south, another to the north, a third towards the west, is supported by twelve stone columns of marvellous size. It has twice four gates, that is four entrances, through three firmly built walls which break upon the pathways in a straight line, of which four means of exit look to the north-east, while the other four look to the south-east. In the middle of the interior of this round house is a round cabin cut out in one and the same rock, in which thrice three men can pray standing; and from the head of a man of ordinary stature as he stands, up to the arch of that small house, a foot and a half is measured upwards.

The entrance of this little cabin looks to the east, and the whole outside is covered with choice marble, while its highest point is adorned with gold, and supports a golden cross of no small size. In the northern part of this cabin is the Sepulchre of the Lord, cut out in the same rock in the inside, but the pavement of the cabin is lower than the place of the Sepulchre; for from its pavement up to the edge of the side of the Sepulchre a measure of about three palms is reckoned. Here we must refer to the difference of names between the Tomb and the Sepulchre; for that round cabin which we have often mentioned, the Evangelists called by another name, the Tomb: they speak of the stone rolled to its mouth, and rolled back from its mouth, when the Lord rose.

That place in the cabin is properly called the Sepulchre, which is in the northern side of the Tomb, in which the body of the Lord, when buried, rested, rolled in the linen cloths: the length of which Arculf measured with his own hand and found to be seven feet. Now this Sepulchre is not, as some think, double, having a projection left from the solid rock, parting and separating the two legs and the two thighs, but is wholly single, affording a bed capable of holding a man lying on his back from his head even to his soles. It is in the manner of a cave, having its opening at the side, and opposite the south part of the sepulchral chamber. The low roof is artificially wrought above it. In the Sepulchre there are further twelve lamps according to the number of the twelve Apostles, always burning day and night, four of which are placed down below in the lowest part of the sepulchral bed, while the other twice four are placed higher above its edge on the right hand; they shine brightly, being nourished with oil.

The Holy Sepulcher, 1789
Buck Whaley

It may be necessary also to remark, that this magnificent church has, at different periods, been known under various denominations. It was first called "Basilica Constantiniana," evidently from the name of its founder; afterwards "New Jerusalem," the "Church of the Cross," the "Church of the Holy Sepulchre," the "Golgothan Church," and last of all the "Temple of the Resurrection."

Probably it still retains the form in which it was first built by Constantine, as the foundations must have been originally dug at a vast expense and labour. Though the temple has been exposed at different periods to the violent attacks of man, the most positive orders having been issued for its demolition by Chorac, king of Persia, in 614, and by Kakem [al-Hakim bi-Amr Illah], Calif of Egypt, four hundred years afterwards yet some parts resisted their barbarous efforts and survived the general devastation which their soldiery spread through the city. Those parts which are coeval with Constantine may be easily distinguished from those of a later date.

The different parts of this church are splendidly lighted by tapers and an amazing number of silver lamps, and at particular times there are several lamps of solid gold used in the Holy Sepulchre. These are all presents from the different Roman Catholic princes; and I have been assured that the plate belonging to the Temple of the Resurrection was worth upwards of one hundred thousand pounds.

While we were in the Greek Church a priest was delivering a sermon. He spoke with much vehemence and energy, and seemed to command the attention of a very large assembly, composed mostly of women; they were all veiled, as the Turks will not permit even the Greek women to appear abroad with their faces uncovered. The concourse of people, always formed at this church, gives it more the appearance of a court of justice than the sacred place of divine worship. The number of different sects, too, which we saw here is really surprising; the Jews only are forbidden to enter the Temple.

Babel in the Cathedral, 1895
Pierre Loti

Oh! the unexpected, the unforgettable impression, the first time one enters that place! A labyrinth of dark sanctuaries of all possible epochs, all conceivable styles, all interconnected by bays, porticoes, superb colonnades; or by tiny furtive doors, ventilation-shafts, holes linking caves. Some chapels are raised, like high tribunes where one catches sight of groups of women in vague recesses, draped in long veils; others are underground, where one pushes past shadowy figures, between expanses of wall still intact, but oozing and black. All this takes place in a crepuscular darkness, only broken by a few brilliant rays of sun which make the surrounding darkness all the gloomier. Everywhere there are tiny silver or gold lamps hanging in their thousands from the vaults. And all around are the crowds, moving en masse as in some sort of Tower of Babel, or else clustered together, roughly sorted by nationality around the various golden tabernacles where Mass is being said.

The Church of the Nativity, 1872
Amy Fullerton

We afterwards walked to the Church of the Nativity. It is now within convent walls, the Armenian, Greek, and Latin creeds each having a portion in it. The position of the church is fine. On a terrace, it overlooks a great expanse of fertile country, and those shepherd-plains which were the scene of the heavenly vision to the watchers over their flocks below. . . .

The crypt of the church, which is evidently an ancient building, is the part to which strangers immediately descend. It presents a series of cavernous recesses, which, by the desire of the monkish guardians, has each its especial title; and over the spot which has been especially chosen to mark the exact situation of the cave where the Nativity took place, are suspended a silver star and lamp. That the hostelry anciently stood here, and that horses and cattle were constantly stabled in the hollows and recesses of the overhanging mountain brow, are facts which require no stretch of belief, and render this actually a probable locality for the birth of our Lord, whose parents sought what shelter could be found in an overcrowded inn, and whose first bed was a manger. But whilst there is this unity of belief below, it is sad to see the neglect of the fine nave of the church above. It is left in utter carelessness and desolation, its magnificent columns bearing witness to its former grandeur; but now it does not appear possible that the three creeds who claim the crypt could join together in preserving the floor of the nave from the commonest desecration of oriental dust and dirt.

The Armenian Convent, 1849–50
Gustave Flaubert

The Armenian convent is massive: it's clean, tidily built, impressive with its interior courtyards, its terraces and stairways. Some buildings for the monks, others for the pilgrims. The Armenians strike me as powerful in an Oriental way: proprietary frivolities speaking of full bellies, such as wrought iron bannisters and terraces. The church is surprising in its richness, its bad taste that nearly achieves majesty . . . walls covered in blue ceramic tiles as high as a man, square columns. On the left, a chapel where a circle marks the spot where St James was beheaded; under the sort of altar surrounded by flowers and torches, a glass case with a severed head . . .

Mostly bad paintings: portraits of patriarchs, under scenes from the life of Jesus, Holy Virgins with the *bambino*, all with silver haloes. In a metal frame, a painted figure with a real diamond on its finger. A painting of St Stephen being stoned with a positively grotesque ferocity, those are real "mean" people. Nearby, a lion devours some saint or other, it's really quite good; his mouth is bigger than the rest of his body. . . . The Armenian church is full of fantasy, garlanded with long strings of ostrich eggs cascading from the ceiling.

Muslim Holy Places

We have selected descriptions of the two sacred mosques by three very different Muslim travelers, the famous Ibn Battuta, the cosmopolitan Ottoman Evliya Çelebi, and the native Jerusalemite al-Muqaddasi. Sadly, but perhaps not

surprisingly, descriptions by Christian travelers tend to be inaccurate and sometimes unsympathetic.

After the Reconquest, c. 1325
Ibn Battuta

We then reached Jerusalem (may God ennoble her!), third in excellence after the two holy shrines of Mecca and Medina and the place whence the Prophet was caught up into heaven. Its walls were destroyed by the illustrious King Saladin and his Successors, for fear lest the Christians should seize it and fortify themselves in it. The sacred mosque is a most beautiful building, and is said to be the largest mosque in the world. Its length from east to west is put at 752 "royal" cubits and its breadth at 435. On three sides it has many entrances, but on the south side I know of one only, which is that by which the imam enters. The entire mosque is an open court and unroofed, except the mosque al-Aqsa, which has a roof of most excellent workmanship, embellished with gold and brilliant colours. Some other parts of the mosque are roofed as well. The Dome of the Rock is a building of extraordinary beauty, solidity, elegance, and singularity of shape. It stands on an elevation in the centre of the mosque and is reached by a flight of marble steps. It has four doors.

The space round it is also paved with marble, excellently done, and the interior likewise. Both outside and inside the decoration is so magnificent and the workmanship so surpassing as to defy description. The greater part is covered with gold so that the eyes of one who gazes on its beauties are dazzled by its brilliance, now glowing like a mass of light, now flashing like lightning. In the centre of the Dome is the blessed rock from which the Prophet ascended to heaven, a great rock projecting about a man's height, and underneath it there is a cave the size of a small room, also of a man's height, with steps leading down to it. Encircling the rock are two railings of excellent workmanship, the one nearer the rock being artistically constructed in iron and the other of wood.

A Light-Filled Mosque, AD 972

al-Muqaddasi

The Masjid al Aksa [the Further Mosque] lies at the south-eastern corner of the Holy City. The stones of its foundations (of the outer wall), which were laid by David, are ten ells, or a little less in length. They are chiselled, finely faced, and jointed, and of hardest material. On these the Khalif 'Abd al Malik subsequently built, using smaller but well-shaped stones, and battlements are added above. This mosque is even more beautiful than that of Damascus, for during the building of it they had for a rival and as a comparison the great church belonging to the Christians at Jerusalem, and they built this to be even more magnificent than that other.

But in the days of the Abbasides occurred the earthquakes which threw down most of the main building; all, in fact, except that portion round the Mihrab. Now when the Khalifa of that day obtained news of this, he enquired and learned that the sum at that time in the treasury would in no wise suffice to restore the mosque. So he wrote to the Governors of the Provinces

Celebi Mehemet Effendi
Ambassadeur extraordinaire du grand Sultan
Achmet 2.ᵉ Empereur des Turcs.

Il a été envoié au Roy Louis 15. pour le féli-
citer sur son avènement a la Couronne de
France a eu audience publique du Roy le 21 Mars
1721.
a Paris Chez Crepy rue S.Jacques au Lion d'argent.

and to other Commanders, that each should undertake the building of a colonnade. The order was carried out, and the edifice rose firmer and more substantial than ever it had been in former times. The more ancient portion remained, even like a beauty spot, in the midst of the new; and it extends as far as the limit of the marble columns, for, beyond, where the columns are of concrete, the later part commences.

The main building of the mosque has twenty-six doors. The door opposite to the Mihrab is called Bab an Nahas al A'tham [the Great Brasen Gate]; it is plated with gilded brass, and is so heavy that only a man strong of shoulder and of arm can turn it on its hinges. To the right hand of the Great Gate are seven large doors, the midmost one of which is covered with gilt plates; and after the same manner there are seven doors to the left. And further, on the eastern side are eleven doors, unornamented. Over the first-mentioned doors, fifteen in number, is a colonnade supported on marble pillars, lately erected by 'Abd Allah ibn Tahir. In the court of the mosque, on the right-hand side, are colonnades supported by marble pillars and pilasters; and on the further side are halls, vaulted in stone. The centre part of the main building of the mosque is covered by a mighty roof, high pitched and gable-wise, behind which rises a magnificent dome. The ceiling everywhere, with the exception of that of the halls on the further side of the court, is formed of lead in sheets, but in these halls the ceilings are faced with mosaics studded in.

The al-Aqsa Mosque, 1648
Evliya Çelebi

It is a large, light-filled mosque, 300 feet in length from the qibla gate to the prayer-niche. . . . Inside are seventy large and small columns of porphyriy, etc., both artificial and natural. Each column is a jewel in itself, worth an Egyptian treasure. . . . As to the prayer-niche, it is profusely gilded, as if it were a lapis-lazuli enamel work studded with jewels. Whatever of precious metals or stones is known on earth has been carved like bird's eyes and inserted by the accomplished master into that jewel-like niche of indescribable beauty. . . .

When one visits the Aqsa Mosque, one comes first to the prayer-niche of [the Caliph] Umar, in the east corner, where he performed his prayers during a whole week after the conquest. Next is the prayer-niche of David, where prayers used to be offered while the foundations were dug. To the left of it, on a stand, is the ancient Koran in the handwriting of [the Caliph] Uthman, in Kufic characters, as though written by the Hand of Power. One visits next the Station of Jesus, to the right of the pulpit; it is a praying-place behind a well-wrought iron grill and has a separate entrance. Finally one comes to the Station of Hizir [St. George] on the left side of the mosque. God be praised, I visited all of them and offered at each two prostrations beseeching their intercession.

The Dome of the Rock, 1648
Evliya Çelebi

They embellished the noble city and the elegant Rock to such an extent that the [Quranic] verse *These are the gardens of Eden, enter and dwell there forever* (cf. 39:73) was justly written over the Gate of Paradise of the noble Rock.

Verily, it is a replica of a pavilion in Paradise. This humble one has travelled for thirty-eight years through seventeen empires and has viewed countless buildings, but I have never seen one that so resembled paradise. When a person enters, he stands dumbfounded and amazed, with finger to mouth. . . .

Through the railing one perceives a flat rock, called the Holy Rock (*Sakhrat Allah*, lit. Rock of God). . . . The late Sultan Ahmed (I, reg. 1603–17) had a richly gilt canopy made, the cover of which was a curtain studded with gold and jewels, and fastened it to the surrounding columns to make a baldachin over the Rock. From this baldachin to the highest point of the dome is a height of 40 or 50 cubits. The interior of this indigo-coloured dome is covered over its whole surface with gold, studded with precious stones set in enamel. The one who painted all four sides is the painter known as Shah Quli.

The Holy Rock, AD 972

al-Muqaddasi

In the centre of the platform is the Dome of the Rock, which rises above an octagonal building having four gates, one opposite to each of the flights of Steps leading up from the court. These four are, the Kiblah [or Southern] Gate, the Gate of Israfil [to the east], the Gate As Sidr [or of the Trumpet, to the north], and [the Women's Gate], Bab an Nisi, which last opens towards the west. All these are adorned with gold, and closing each of them is a beautiful door of cedar-wood finely worked in pattern. These last were sent by command of the mother of the Khalif Al Muktadir Billah.

At each of the gates is a balustrade of marble and cedar-wood, with brass-work without; and in the railing, likewise, are gates, but these are unornamented. Within the building are three concentric colonnades, with columns of the most beautiful marble, polished, that can be seen, and above is a low vaulting. Within these again is the central hall over The Rock; the hall is circular, not octagonal, and is surrounded by columns of polished marble supporting round arches. Built above these, and rising high into the air, is the drum in which are large openings; and over the drum is the Dome. The Dome, from the floor up to the pinnacle, which rises into the air, is in height a hundred ells, and from afar off, you may perceive on the summit of the Dome, its beautiful pinnacle, the size of which is a fathom and a span.

The Dome, externally, is completely covered with brass plates, gilt, while the building itself, its floor and its walls, and the drum, both within and without, are ornamented with marble and mosaics, after the manner that we have already described when speaking of the mosque of Damascus. The cupola of the Dome is built in three sections: the inner is of ornamental plates; next come iron beams interlaced, set in free so that the wind may not cause it to shift; and the third casing is of wood, on which are fixed the outer plates. Up through the middle of the cupola goes a passage way, by which a workman may ascend to the pinnacle for aught that may be wanting, or in order to repair the structure. At the dawn, when the light of the sun first strikes on the Cupola, and the Drum catches the rays; then is this edifice a marvellous sight to behold, and one such that in all Islam I have never seen its equal; neither have I heard tell of aught built in pagan times that could rival in grace this Dome of the Rock. . . .

The mosque is served by special attendants; their service was instituted by the Khalif ʿAbd al Malik, the men being chosen from among the Royal Fifth of the Captives taken in War, and hence they are called Al Akhmis [the Quintans]. None besides these are employed in the service, and they take their watch in turn beside The Rock. From Jerusalem come cheeses, cotton, the celebrated raisins of the species known as 'Ainuni and Duri, excellent apples, bananas—which same is a fruit of the form of a cucumber, but the skin peels off and the interior is not unlike the water-melon, only finer flavoured and more luscious—also pine-nuts of the kind called 'Kuraish-Bite,' and its equal is not to be found elsewhere; further—mirrors, lamp-jars, and needles.

Personal Vignettes

After a visit to Washington, DC, the lovable cartoon elephant Babar complained he was "tired of monuments." This section highlights a few personal escapades or non-monumental observations of some of our travelers.

A Fright in the Cave, 1875
Isabel Burton

It was later on in the day [Holy Saturday, 1875], after we had made an excursion to see the Convent of the Cross, that Richard [Burton], Charles Tyrwhitt-Drake, and I went off to explore the Magharat el Kotn, also called the Royal Caverns. They are enormous quarries, the entrance to which looks like a hole in the wall outside Jerusalem, not far from the Gate of Damascus. We crept in, and found ourselves lost in endless artificial caves and galleries. Richard and Mr. Drake were delighted with them; but I soon left the enthusiasts, for the caves did not interest me. I had kept Lent fasting; I had attended all the long ceremonies of Holy Week; and I was therefore very tired on this day, Holy Saturday, the more so because I had not only attended my own Church's ceremonies, but all those of every sect in Jerusalem. So I gave up exploring the caves, and sauntered away to the northernmost point of Mount Bezetha, and saw the Cave of the Prophet Jeremias. It was here that he wrote his Lamentations.

I then climbed up to a large cave somewhat to the left, above that of Jeremias, where I could look down upon Jerusalem. Here, worn out with fatigue, fasting, and over-excitement, I lay down with my head upon the stone, and slept a long sleep of two hours, during which time I dreamed a long, vivid dream. Its details in full would occupy a volume. . . . The spirit of Jeremias might have touched the stone upon which I slept, or Baruch might have dwelt there. I dreamed for hours, and then I awoke. A goat-herd had entered the cave, and I half fancy he had shaken me, for he looked scared and said, "Pardon, Ya Sitti; I thought you were dead."

The bells of the Sepulchre were giving out their deep-tongued notes and re-echoing over the hills. I looked at my watch; it was the Ave Maria—sunset. I came back with a rush to reality; all my dream views vanished, and the castles in the air tumbled down like a pack of cards. Nothing remained of my wondrous dream, with its mar-vellous visions, its stately procession of emperors, kings, queens, pontiffs, and ministers—nothing remained of them all, but only my poor, humble self, private and obscure, still to toil on and pray and suffer. I had to rouse myself at once, and almost to run, so as to pass the gates before I was locked out of the city for the night. No one would have thought of looking for me in that cave. I should certainly have been reported as murdered. . . .

The next morning, Easter Sunday, I was up before dawn, and had the happiness of hearing two Masses and receiving Holy Communion in the Sepulchre. I was the only person present besides the celebrant and the acolyte. During the day we walked round about Jerusalem, and visited many sacred spots.

On Easter Monday in the afternoon we rode over bad country to the Cave of St. John the Baptist, where he led the life of a hermit and prepared for his preaching. It was a small cave, and there is a bench in it cut in the stone, which served the Baptist as a bed. The priests now celebrate Mass on it.

Mark Twain in Jerusalem, 1869
Bertha Spafford Vester

Among the many tourists whom Mr. Floyd conducted through the Holy Land was Mark Twain. The famous author rode a horse he named Baalbek, because he was such a "magnificent ruin." *Innocents Abroad* was written after this trip. Mr. Floyd used to amuse us by telling us anecdotes about Mark Twain. I remember one special story which, as far as I know, has never been published. The party was camping in Galilee, where in the spring of the year the wild flowers are plentiful and very beautiful. Herbs and plants grow to abnormal size but retain their luscious and tender qualities. The cook had gathered some wild greens and made a salad which was served with roast lamb for dinner. A member of the party asked the author why he was like Nebuchadnezzar, and expected the answer to be because he was eating the "grass of the field." Mark Twain promptly replied "because I am eating with the brutes."

An Imperial Journey, 1898
Estelle Blyth

It was one of the hottest Octobers we had had for years, and October is one of our worst months. The Kaiser did not seem to feel the heat but the poor Kaiserin and the suite did. As for the horses—those splendidly plucky little Palestine animals which are game to the last and then drop, literally, in harness—well, he killed over forty of them, and they were left lying along the route taken by this "Crusader." All through the heat of the day the party travelled. The poor Kaiserin arrived in Jerusalem positively worn out with the two days' journey. She was only just recovering from the effects of a very drastic anti-fat treatment, which the Kaiser had invented and insisted on her trying. Her ladies complained quite openly of this, and declared that the Kaiser had very nearly killed their mistress. She was certainly charmingly slender, but very far from strong; her manner was sweet and gracious, and she was both handsome and stately on occasion.

Her ladies wore very rich silk dresses, with striped white cotton stockings and elastic-sided boots. It was strange to behold these survivals of a day which, till then, we had imagined to have vanished with the crinoline.

The Kaiser had long before announced his intention of entering Jerusalem on horseback. This whim of his worried the Turkish authorities very much, for according to the old tradition only the Conqueror may ride through the Gates of the Holy City. Between their genuine desire to be polite to a guest, even a rather trying and exacting guest, and their determination to run no risks with old traditions, which have a way of coming true, the Turks, as usual, fell back upon compromise. They broke down a bit of the beautiful fifteenth-century wall of Jerusalem, leaving a gap wide enough for the procession to pass through in all its dignity. So the Emperor did enter Jerusalem riding—but not through a Gate; and Jerusalem ceased to be a walled-in City. The Kaiserin and her ladies drove in open carriages. A few rather haphazard decorations had been put up here and there in the streets, and Jerusalem turned out in its best clothes to welcome the Imperial visitors.

The Kaiser had designed for himself and his suite a buff-coloured uniform; he wore a sun-helmet with a military turn to it, and a long white silk *burnouse,* or mantle, which was carefully spread out over the horse's hind-quarters. . . . Eastern crowds do not cheer, but the Kaiser seemed well satisfied with his reception. Like Godfrey de Bouillon—but how different!—he went straight to the Church of the Holy Sepulchre.

Russian Pilgrims, 1907
Gertrude Bell

At the foot of the first descent there is a spring, *'Ain esh Shems,* the Arabs call it, the Fountain of the Sun, but the Christian pilgrims have named it the Apostles' Well. In the winter you will seldom pass there without seeing some Russian peasants resting on their laborious way up from Jordan. Ten thousand of them pour yearly into the Holy Land, old men and women, for the most part, who have pinched and saved all their life long to lay together the £30 or so which carry them to Jerusalem. From the furthest ends of the Russian empire they come on foot to the Black Sea, where they take ship as deck passengers on board a dirty little Russian boat. The pilgrims reach Jerusalem before Christmas and stay till after Easter that they may light their tapers at the sacred fire that breaks out from the Sepulchre on the morning of the Resurrection.

They wander on foot through all the holy places, lodging in big hostels built for them by the Russian Government. Many die from exposure and fatigue and the unaccustomed climate; but to die in Palestine is the best of favours that the Divine hand can bestow, for their bones rest softly in the Promised Land and their souls fly straight to Paradise.

I heard in Jerusalem a story which is a better illustration of their temper than pages of description. It was of a man who had been a housebreaker and had been caught in the act and sent to Siberia, where he did many years of penal servitude. But when his time was up he came home to his old mother with a changed heart, and they two set out together for the Holy Land that he might make expiation for his sins. Now at the season when the pilgrims are in Jerusalem, the riff-raff of Syria congregates there to cheat their simplicity and pester them for alms, and one of these vagabonds came and begged of the Russian penitent at a time when he had nothing to give. The Syrian, enraged at his refusal, struck the other to the earth and injured him so severely that he was in hospital for three months.

When he recovered his consul came to him and said, "We have got the man who nearly killed you; before you leave you must give evidence against him." But the pilgrim answered, "No, let him go. I too am a criminal."

A Franco–French Experience, 1806–1807
François-René de Chateaubriand

On returning from my visit to the Sepulchres of the Kings, I passed through the valley of Jehoshaphat: the sun was setting behind Jerusalem; he gilded with his last rays this mass of ruins and the mountains of Judea. I sent back my companions by the gate of St. Stephen, keeping nobody but the janissary with me. Seating myself at the foot of the tomb of Jehoshaphat, with my face towards the Temple, I took a volume of Racine from my pocket and read Athaliah. At these first verses *Oui, je viens dans son Temple adorer l'Eternel, &c.* [Yes, to your Temple I come, to worship the Eternal One] It is impossible for me to express what I felt. I fancied that I could hear the songs of Solomon and the voices of the Prophets; ancient Jerusalem rose to my view; the shades of Joad, Athaliah, and Josabeth issued from the tomb; and it seemed as if I had been incapable till that moment of appreciating the genius of Racine. What poetry! since I thought it worthy of the place where I was. The pen drops from my fingers: one feels ashamed to scribble any more after a man has written such verses. . . .

I had seen every thing at Jerusalem; I was acquainted with the interior and exterior of that city, and better acquainted with them than with the interior of Paris and its vicinity: I began, therefore, to think of my departure. The Fathers of the Holy Land determined to confer on me an honour which I had neither solicited nor deserved. In consideration of the feeble services which, as they said, I had rendered to religion, they requested me to accept the Order of the Holy Sepulchre. . . . We left the convent at one o'clock and repaired to the church of the Holy Sepulchre. We went into the chapel belonging to the Latin Fathers; the doors were carefully shut, lest the Turks should perceive the arms, which might cost the clergy their lives.

The superior put on his pontifical habits; the lamps and tapers were lighted; all the brethren present formed a circle round me, with their hands folded upon their breasts. While they sung the *Veni Creator* in a low voice, the superior stepped up to the altar, and I fell on my knees at his feet. The spurs and sword of Godfrey de Bouillon were taken out of the treasury of the Holy Sepulchre: two of the monks, standing one on each side of me, held the venerable relics. The superior recited the accustomed prayers and asked me the usual questions: he then put the spurs on my heels and struck me thrice over the shoulders with the sword, on which the monks began to sing the *Te Deum*. . . .

All this is but a shadow of the days that are past. But if it be considered that I was at Jerusalem, in the church of Calvary, within a dozen paces of the tomb of Jesus Christ, and thirty from that of Godfrey de Bouillon; that I was equipped with the spurs of the Deliverer of the Holy Sepulchre and had touched that sword which so noble and so valiant an arm had once wielded. . . . I am a Frenchman; Godfrey de Bouillon was a Frenchman; and his ancient arms, in touching me, communicated an increased ardour for glory and for the honour of my country.

Spiritual Exuberance, Holy Fire, and Cynicism

No anthology of travel writing about Jerusalem could ignore the most spectacular event of the Christian year, the miracle of the Holy Fire. Easter was the prime pilgrimage season, so

*there are dozens of accounts to choose from. We have selected
a Protestant, a Muslim, and the enigmatic Grigorii Rasputin
of Imperial Russian notoriety.*

Disorders in the Cathedral, 1697
Henry Maundrell

We went about midday to fee the function of the Holy
Fire. This is a ceremony kept up by the Greeks, and
Armenians, upon a persuasion, that every Easter Eve,
there is a Miraculous Flame, descends from Heaven
into the Holy Sepulcher, and kindles all the Lamps and
Candles there, as the Sacrifice was burnt at the prayers
of Elijah.

Coming to the Church of the Holy Sepulcher, we
found it crowded with a numerous and distracted Mob,
making a hideous clamour very unfit for that sacred
place, and better becoming Bacchanals than Christians.
Getting with some struggle thro' this crowd, we went up
into the Gallery on that side of the Church next the Latin
Convent whence we could discern all that pass'd in this
religious frenzy.

They began their disorders by running round the holy Sepulcher with all their might and swiftness, crying out as they went, *Huia*, which signifies this is he, or this is it: an expression by which they assert the verity of the Christian Religion. Alter they had by these vertiginous circulations and clamours turn'd their heads, and inflam'd their madness, they began to act the most antick tricks, and postures, in a thousand shapes of distraction. Sometimes they drag'd one another along the floor all round the Sepulcher; sometimes they set one man upright on another's shoulders, and in this posture march'd round; sometimes they took men with their heels upward, and hurry'd them about in such an undecent manner as to expose their Nuditys; sometimes they tumbled round the Sepulcher, after the manner of tumblers on the stage: in a word, nothing can be imagin'd more rude or extravagant than what was acted upon this occasion. . . .

The cause of their pressing in this manner, is the great desire they have, to light their Candles at the holy Flame, as soon as it is first brought out of the Sepulcher: it being esteem'd the most sacred and pure, as coming immediately from Heaven. The two Miracle Mongers had not been above a minute in the Holy Sepulcher, when the glimmering of the holy Fire was seen, or imagined to appear, thro' some chinks of the door, and certainly Bedlam itself never saw such an unruly transport, as was produc'd in the Mob at this light.

Immediately after out came the two Priests, with blazing Torches in their hands, which they held up at the door of the Sepulcher, while the people throng'd about with unexpressible ardour: every one striving to obtain a part of the first, and purest Flame. The Turks in the mean time, with huge Clubs, laid them on without mercy: but all this could not repel them, the excess of their transport making them insensible of pain. Those that got the Fire applied it immediately to their Beards, Faces, and Bosoms, pretending that it would not burn like an Earthly Flame. But I plainly saw none of them could endure this experiment long enough to make good that pretention.

The Holy Fire, 1648
Evliya Çelebi

The reason it burns on their notorious Festival of the Red Egg (Easter) is this: There is a zinc jar concealed in the apogee of the dome. It contains olive oil mixed with a small amount of naphtha. During the days of the festival, because of the heat, the oil in the jar drips down through the highly-wrought chain and fills the lamp, with none of the infidels aware of it. The wall on the eastern side of the Church, above the prayer-niche which is their 'qibla' (ie altar) has been embellished by the clever master builder with panes of crystal and/or glass. At noon on the Red Egg days, the glass panes get very hot from the beating of the sun. This heat in turn affects the large lamp, which bursts into flame.

If the weather happens to be cloudy on those days, and the sun is not strong enough to produce this effect, one of the clever monks secretly climbs on top of the dome and kindles the oil mixed with naphtha at the tip of the chain. The fire runs down the chain, in plain view of the infidels standing below, who think that it is fire from heaven. Awestruck, they remove their hats and cry *Kireleys, Kireleys!* [*Kyrie eleison*].

In this manner the fire of Nimrod descends into that lamp and lights up the interior of the Church. The monks use the fire in the lamp to kindle the thousands of lamps that the infidels have in their hands, and the infidels in turn take those nefarious camphor candles and distribute the fire throughout the Christian world. Vast sums are earned from this trade as well. It is indeed a strange art of the lamp.

Easter Fervor and Renewal, 1911
Grigorii Rasputin

O, such a feeling of expectation, for the holy fire, as all worshippers thirst for the Procession of the Cross! They have been waiting for this more than a day, thousands of people from a host of nations. Many are crying; Arabs are clapping, jumping, and singing something in a state of frenzy, while all around stand Turkish troops and *kavasy*. The moment arrives: the patriarch removes his outer clothing, remaining only in his underwear, and enters the Kuvukliya, where the sepulchre of Christ is.

The people, crying and all worked up, wait for the patriarch to emerge with the fire. . . . He leaps out carrying the fire, and runs to the Church of the Resurrection, lights the inextinguishable candles, then appears before the people. From his bundle of candles the pilgrims light their candles with great fervor. Everyone is energized and beside himself with joy. They light their candles all at once—thirty-three candles. The pilgrims' faces glow with incredible joy, and a loud noise is heard throughout the temple. The people are filled with utmost joy and with grace, by the lighting of the candles from the holy fire. Some take the fire home, others only burn candles, up to three times they light and extinguish them. A miraculous event took place, and is taking place. O God, give us memory that we will not forget such renewal!

Street Life, Seasons,
and Celebration

For all its celestial status, Jerusalem is an earthly city, where the rains come, or fail to, and it gets deathly cold in winter and furnace-hot in summer. Rubbish must be removed (or not), as

with any other city. The seasons provide a progression of liturgi-
cal celebrations, some of which cross religious boundaries and
provide a rare opportunity for peaceful intercourse.

A Cleansing Rain, c. AD 670
Arculfus

On the fifteenth day of the month of September yearly,
an almost countless multitude of various nations is in the
habit of gathering from all sides to Jerusalem for the purposes of commerce by mutual sale and purchase. Whence
it necessarily happens that crowds of various nations stay
in that hospitable city for some days, while the very great
number of their camels and horses and asses, not to speak
of mules and oxen, for their varied baggage, strews the
streets of the city here and there with the abominations of
their excrements: the smell of which brings no ordinary
nuisance to the citizens and even makes walking difficult.

Wonderful to say, on the night after the day of departure with the various beasts of burden of the crowds,
an immense abundance of rain falls from the clouds on
that city, which washes all the abominable filths from

the streets, and cleanses it from the uncleannesses. For the very situation of Jerusalem, beginning from the northern brow of Mount Sion, has been so disposed by its Founder, God, on a lofty declivity, sloping down to the lower ground of the northern and eastern walls that that overabundance of rain cannot settle at all in the streets, like stagnant water, but rushes down, like rivers, from the higher to the lower ground and further this inundation of the waters of heaven, flowing through the eastern gates, and bearing with it all the filthy abominations, enters the Valley of Josaphat and swells the torrent of Cedron: and after having thus baptized Jerusalem, this overabundance of rain always ceases.

The Pilgrimage Season, 1844
Alexander William Kinglake

The pilgrims begin to arrive in Palestine some weeks before the Easter festival of the Greek Church. They come from Egypt, from all parts of Syria, from Armenia and Asia Minor, from Stamboul, from Roumelia, from the provinces of the Danube, and from all the Russias.

Most of these people bring with them some articles of merchandise, but I myself believe (notwithstanding the common taunt against pilgrims) that they do this rather as a means of paying the expenses of their journey, rather than from a spirit of mercenary speculation. . . .

The space fronting the Church of the Holy Sepulchre soon becomes a kind of bazaar, or rather, perhaps, reminds you of an English fair. . . . I have never, I think, seen elsewhere in Asia so much commercial animation as upon this square of ground by the church door; the "money-changers" seemed to be almost as brisk and lively as if they had been *within* the Temple. . . .

The enthusiasm that had glowed, or seemed to glow, within me, for one blessed moment, when I knelt by the shrine of the Virgin at Nazareth, was not rekindled at Jerusalem. In the stead of the solemn gloom and the deep stillness rightfully belonging to the Holy City, there was the hum and the bustle of active life. It was the "height of the season." The Easter ceremonies drew near; the pilgrims were flocking in from all quarters, and although their objects were partly at least of a religious character, yet their "arrivals" brought as much stir and liveliness to the city as though they had come up to marry their daughters.

Seasonal Feasts, AD 972
al-Muqaddasi

Of Christian Feasts that are observed also by the Muslims of Syria, for the division of the seasons of the year, are the following: Easter, at the New Year (old style, the Vernal Equinox); Whitsuntide, at the time of heat; Christmas, at the time of cold; the Feast of St. Barbara in the rainy season—and the people have a proverb, which says, "When St. Barbara's Feast comes round, then the mason may take to his flute," meaning that he may then sit quiet at home; the Feast of the Kalends, and again, one of their proverbs is, "When the Kalends come, keep warm and stay at home;" the Feast of the Cross at the time of grape-gathering; and the Feast of Lydda at the time of sowing the seed.

Drought in the Holy City, 1855

James Finn

The close of 1855 was marked by a distressing lack of rain, which raised food to famine prices. Wheat was as dear as it had been in the scarcity of 1854, and rice was double the ordinary price. The early rains expected in October and November had been almost wholly wanting, and it was, therefore, impossible to plough and sow the winter crop of grain, as usual at that season.

The distress rose to such a pitch, not only among the Jews, whose sufferings are at all times pitiable, but amongst the natives of other classes, and even among the Moslems, that the Pasha early in November invited a Council of Consuls to advise as to what should be done. The advice given was to sell at a moderate price some of the surplus corn in the Government stores. A few hours of rain, however, raised hopes that the trouble would soon be at an end, but instead of this another month of drought and warm weather followed. The want of water now became serious, more especially in the Jewish quarter, where the house cisterns, being mostly out of repair, do not hold enough for even a few weeks' supply of the year.

At last the state of things was so serious that the Moslem Effendis, headed by the Pasha, walked in procession (of course having their shoes off) round the dome of the Rock, in connection with the offering of special prayers to Almighty God for the blessing of rain. This we ourselves beheld, looking down from the Mount of Olives upon the Sanctuary in Moriah. The Jews had for some time been observing strict fasts with prayer in the synagogues. The Christians, too, took their part in the supplications.

But still there was no rain. At last the Pasha sent a message to the Jews, offering them free entrance into the Temple Sanctuary, in order that they might pray at the Sacred Rock for rain. The Jews declined this from religious motives, but requested to be allowed to pray at the Tomb of David, which was granted for the afternoon of December 17. Rain began to fall before the hour came, and continued for several hours, a fine rainbow spanning the north of the city before the sun went down.

One must have lived in an Eastern climate, where the rains cease, as a matter of course, during the summer months, to understand the intense feeling of relief with which those few hours of rain were welcomed after the anxieties of two months in which the rain had been delayed. But even now the supply was inadequate. The weather became cold and bright, and the ground was still parched and the wells were empty.

At last on January 6th rain fell in earnest.

The Eastern Christians in their joy ascribed the blessing coming at last to a circumstance that had occurred the same day. The Pasha had a few days before visited and inspected our church. Before leaving our premises he expressed his intention of attending Divine service on the next Sunday morning. This he did, remaining till the close of the Litany, having our prayer-book in Turkish placed ready for his use. . . .

The day was Epiphany Day. What was the joy of the whole city to see clouds gathering round, and before the Pasha could reach home the rain came down and rapidly increased. The Christian natives said the rain came because the Pasha had prayed in the church. Next day the ground was covered with snow, which for agricultural purposes is always regarded as a blessing even greater than that of rain.

Muslim Feast Celebrations, 1900
Bertha Spafford Vester

The Nebi Musa Celebration. Many who could not afford carriages rode on donkeys, horses, mules, and camels. . . . [Now we do not] have the many kinds of dervishes who lent so much colour to the celebration when I was a child. They came to Jerusalem especially for the Prophet's feast and procession. Some ate live coals, others forced spikes through their cheeks. Snake charmers came from Upper Egypt.

During this particular procession, when I was five or six, I was walking along unconscious of fear when I realized I was alone. Father and Mother were busy with their guests and Hannieh had stopped to chat with some Arab friends. It is one thing to watch such a scene from a safe distance and another to be in the midst of it. Suddenly I found myself walking in the procession surrounded by one of the village bands. Over me towered fierce-looking men carrying banners, and others were pounding on large and small drums, while others were making a terrific clashing with their cymbals. Amidst these were dervishes twirling round and round in religious frenzy, their bushy hair sticking out all over their heads, their eyes rolling, and spikes sticking through their cheeks.

I did not cry—for once I was too frightened to cry. I just stood petrified, and suddenly, pushing through the hysterical crowd to my rescue, came my tall, dark, kindly friend, Abu Nassib. Oh, how glad I was to see him.

Eid al-Fitr. Then came the three days' feast at the end of Ramadan, which is the month of fasting. In those days it was the custom to picnic in the open fields outside Herod's Gate, where the American School of Oriental Research now stands. No buildings were there then, only level fields and a few sparse olive trees. Merry-go-rounds and swings were erected for this celebration, and there were peep-shows—many exhibiting obscene pictures—and hawkers who made a roaring business selling Damascus sweetmeats and Shar el Banat (maiden's hair), candy shredded so fine it resembled hair, and Lahit el Halkum (Turkish delight), and salted and roasted watermelon and pumpkin seeds, and, in season, green and roasted chickpeas tied in bunches. There was sus (liquorice water) and pink lemonade in brightly decorated receptacles, served in shallow brass cups. Venders used these like cymbals in a dexterous rhythm to attract customers. Gypsies, notorious fortunetellers, in their gay costumes gathered there from neighbouring countries.

The scene resembled an old-time country fair. . . . The people wore their best clothes and spent lavishly the savings stored up for the occasion. Crowds of women were kaleidoscopic in their brightly coloured izzars, or outer street costumes, and the bright parasols they loved added colour to the already gay picture.

Horse racing was the chief attraction. Arabs do not have our idea of competitive racing. The gaily-bedecked horses rushed madly around the field, while their excited riders dug in their spurs. Some of the horses' trappings were really beautiful, with silver-mounted bridles and gaudy tassels, and some even had ostrich feathers fastened to their heads. The wilder the horse and rider became, the more the spectators enjoyed the race. There were no cups or prizes, and the only award was a handkerchief tied to the horse's bridle. The winner, generally the most reckless rider, carried off the greatest number of handkerchiefs. Especially imported cheap but highly coloured handkerchiefs or veils were sold in the crowd to award the riders.

Spring in Jerusalem, 1860
Mary Eliza Rogers

I found Jerusalem in the early spring altogether different to Jerusalem in the hot summer time, when it had often appeared to me, literally, "a city of stone, in a land of iron, with a sky of brass," and when at midday all unsheltered places were quite deserted, and those people who could do so, lived in tents in olive-groves in the valleys or on the hills round about Jerusalem. Now all was changed. The few open spaces within the city walls were green with grass, or patches of wheat and barley, and the whole of the mosque inclosure was like meadow-land sprinkled with flowers. The very walls were garnished with rough leaves, stonecrop, pellitory and bright blossoms. Among them the bitter hyssop and bright yellow henbane were pointed out to me, growing luxuriantly on the Tower of Hippicus, in the dry moat, and on all the most ancient buildings; while out of the cracks of the domes, and on the terraced roofs of many of the houses, straggling herbage sprang.

In the streets there was renewed activity, for already the Latin pilgrims were beginning to flock to Jerusalem

that they might celebrate Easter at the Holy Sepulchre. English and American travellers were to be seen
in the principal streets, sketching under difficulties in
the midst of crowds of lookers-on, or making bad bar-
gains with the turbaned salesmen in the bazaars. Outside the town, too, the scenery had changed. Wherever
the earth rested on the rocky hills, verdure appeared,
and the plains, and the cemeteries and valleys, were
gay with flowers. Bulbous plants abounded, especially
asphodels, and the hyacinth, squill, garlic, and star of
Bethlehem. Every evening at sunset large companies of
people of all tribes and nations might be seen entering
the city gates after having enjoyed their evening walk. . . .

Politics, Consuls, and Dignitaries

All foreign powers of any stature or would-be stature were repre-
sented by their Consul; during late Ottoman times these officials
had ambassadorial status, receiving and protecting visitors of
their nationality. The Great Powers all had chosen minorities
which they undertook to protect through intercession with the

Sublime Porte. This relationship also provided the respective Powers with a pretext to interfere in Ottoman affairs—ostensibly on their protégés' behalf. All accurately put in context by none other than Karl Marx.

The Geopolitical Dimension, 1854
Karl Marx

Parts of the Holy Places and of the Church of the Holy Sepulcher are possessed by the Latins, the Greeks, the Armenians, the Abyssinians, the Syrians, and the Copts. Between all these diverse pretendents there originated a conflict. The sovereigns of Europe who saw, in this religious quarrel, a question of their respective influences in the Orient, addressed themselves in the first instance to the masters of the soil, to fanatic and greedy Pashas, who abused their position. The Ottoman Porte and its agents . . . gave judgment in turns favorable to the Latins, Greeks, and Armenians, asking and receiving gold from all hands, and laughing at each of them.

Hardly had the Turks granted a *firman* [decree], acknowledging the right of the Latins to the possession of a contested place, when the Armenians presented themselves with a heavier purse, and instantly obtained a contradictory *firman*. . . .There is no sanctuary, no chapel, no stone of the Church of the Holy Sepulcher, that had been left unturned for the purpose of constituting a quarrel between the different Christian communities.

Around the Holy Sepulcher we find an assemblage of all the various sects of Christianity, behind the religious pretensions of whom are concealed as many political and national rivalries. Jerusalem and the Holy Places are inhabited by nations professing religions: the Latins, the Greeks, Armenians, Copts, Abyssinians, and Syrians. . . .

Imagine all these conflicting peoples beleaguering the Holy Sepulcher, the battle conducted by the monks, and the ostensible object of their rivalry being a star from the grotto of Bethlehem, a tapestry, a key of a sanctuary, an altar, a shrine, a chair, a cushionany ridiculous precedence!

The quarrels between churchmen are the most venomous, said Mazarin. Now fancy these churchmen, who not only have to live upon, but live in, these sanctuaries together! To finish the picture, be it remembered that the fathers of the Latin Church, almost exclusively composed of Romans, Sardinians, Neapolitans, Spaniards and Austrians, are all of them jealous of the French protectorate, and would like to substitute that of Austria, Sardinia or Naples, the Kings of the two latter countries both assuming the title of King of Jerusalem. . . . The Mussulmans, forming about a fourth part of the whole, and consisting of Turks, Arabs and Moors, are, of course, the masters in every respect, as they are in no way affected with the weakness of their Government at Constantinople. . . .

It will now be understood why the common worship of the Christians at the Holy Places resolves itself into a continuance of desperate Irish rows between the diverse sections of the faithful; but that, on the other hand, these sacred rows merely conceal a profane battle, not only of nations but of races; and that the Protectorate of the Holy Places which appears ridiculous to the Occident but all important to the Orientals is one of the phases of the Oriental question incessantly reproduced, constantly stifled, but never solved.

A Son Is Born to Napoleon III, 1856
James Finn

Thus [a cannon salvo] was announced to the varied population and to all the pilgrims in the city (for it was drawing towards Easter, and pilgrims and travellers were arriving in considerable numbers) that there was born the Prince Imperial of France, heir to the Emperor Louis Napoleon Buonaparte. The French mail had brought the tidings at daybreak.

Visits of congratulation (in uniform) were of course paid at the French Consulate, and arrangements made for illumination of the British Consulate at night, and for entertainment of the French Consul with his staff and all French and English travellers, as also of the Pasha and his suite. Native musicians attended and performed Oriental music on the dulcimer, accompanied with singing. The son of the barber Butros was the chief singer, and he and his fellow performers also gave us a free translation in Arabic of the initial verses of the 'Marseillaise.' . . . In the rests between these performances, some Jews outside the windows, which were filled with lights and garlanded with evergreens, gave us interludes on a kind of bagpipe, with cymbals and a big drum, played without any intelligible time or tune.

It was curious to see the native townspeople with lanterns in hand standing in lines against the opposite walls listening and enjoying the unusual spectacle, watching the kawwas and two Abyssinians who grinned with

delight while keeping up the bonfire and the row of tar fires in pots on the roof.

That evening there was an assembly at the Consulate, perhaps the most extraordinary in its composition that we had ever witnessed under our roof, or indeed in Jerusalem. The ecclesiastical heads of all the various churches were present with their respective suites, including the Latin Patriarch, the Armenian Patriarch and bishops, the Venerable Greek Metropolitan Bishop (his Patriarch being away in Constantinople). The English Bishop had left the day before for Nabloos, but the head of the Jewish Mission, John Nicolayson, and the physician, Dr. Macgowan, were present, as well as ecclesiastics of other nations, among them an Apostle of the Irvingites, and le Pere Ratisbonne (founder of the new order of the *Dames de Sion*), in his clerical dress, and with highly intellectual features; the Turkish Pasha and his suite; the Commandant of the troops with his, and the French Consul with his suite and the French travellers, and a new Spanish Consul-General (the first foreigner appointed to that rank for Jerusalem and newly arrived), Don Fernando de la Vera y Isla. Besides these were a host of travellers and residents of all nations. The high ecclesiastics and officials all wore their decorations—ribands, stars, crosses, and religious insignia—with a profusion of diamonds.

A Bishop's Household, 1914
Estelle Blyth

During our time in Palestine we had servants of all races and of all creeds. At one period the kawass and the stable-boy were Moslems, the cook and the kitchenmaid Beth-lehem women (Greek Orthodox Christians, that is), the housemaid an Armenian, the gate-keeper a Moor, and the gardener as great a rogue as ever came out of the Greek Levant. They all got on excellently together, and the breezes, chiefly on religious topics, though lively at the time, were short and infrequent. I should explain that a kawass is an official manservant, a Moslem, whose pres-ence in the households of patriarchs, bishops, and consuls was obligatory under Turkish law. In the early days he was answerable for the life and safety of his foreign Christian master; latterly, of course, the post was purely formal.

The kawass wore a picturesque uniform, full baggy trousers of scarlet or blue cloth, a bright-coloured silken sash round the waist, and a short jacket and close waistcoat, all embroidered in gold braid. When out with his master or with any members of the household, he wore a long curved scimitar with solid silver handle and a sheath embossed in silver.

Our kawasses spent a good deal of time rubbing up these silver embellishments, but the scimitars were old, and though the blades were beautifully patterned I do not think they could have wounded even a finger very severely. The kawass always walked in front (other servants behind, unless carrying a lantern at night); his business was to clear the way for you, which was a great convenience, for any such thing as a rule of the road for man, beast, or vehicle, never entered into the heads of the Turkish officials nor any one else.

On state or official occasions, such as an exchange of visits between their masters, the kawass of the visiting dignitary would carry, in addition to his scimitar, a long silver-headed staff which he struck upon the ground at regular intervals; the kawasses at the house visited would head the little procession from the carriage to the house, also armed with their official staffs and scimitars. When my sister Grace was married, all the foreign consuls, bishops, and patriarchs sent their kawasses to escort her carriage from the Jaffa Gate to the church door, and she drove in at walking pace preceded by twenty-one of these magnificent beings in uniform, the sound of their staffs brought down at regular intervals in unison being audible for some distance.

Early Twentieth Century

The first twenty years of the last century were not auspicious ones for the Holy City or elsewhere in the Levant. The rivalries and tensions arising from the Eastern Question in the run-up to the First World War were keenly felt in Jerusalem, where the Great Powers vied and jostled with each other.

A Stormy Entrance into Jerusalem, 1907
Gertrude Bell

It was a stormy morning, the 5th of February. The west wind swept up from the Mediterranean, hurried across the plain where the Canaanites waged war with the stubborn hill dwellers of Judaea, and leapt the barrier of mountains to which the kings of Assyria and of Egypt had laid vain siege. It shouted the news of rain to Jerusalem and raced onwards down the barren eastern slopes, cleared the deep bed of Jordan with a bound, and vanished across the hills of Moab into the desert. And all the hounds of the storm followed behind, a yelping pack, coursing eastward and rejoicing as they went. No one with life in his body could stay in on such a day, but for me there was little question of choice.

At nine we were in the saddle, riding soberly round the walls of Jerusalem, down into the valley of Gethsemane, past the garden of the Agony and up on to the Mount of Olives. Here I paused to recapture the impression, which no familiarity can blunt, of the walled city on the hill, grey in a grey and stony landscape under the heavy sky, but illumined by the hope and the unquench-able longing of generations of pilgrims. Human aspira-tion, the blind reaching out of the fettered spirit towards a goal where all desire shall be satisfied and the soul find peace, these things surround the city like a halo, half glo-rious, half pitiful, shining with tears and blurred by many a disillusion.

Wartime Hardship, 1917
Sir Ronald Storrs

Throughout those early days in Jerusalem my chief, my nightmare anxiety, was the scarcity of food amount-ing almost to famine. One morning early in January I became aware of a crying and a screaming beneath my office window. I looked out on a crowd of veiled Arab women, some of whom tore their garments apart to reveal the bones almost piercing their skin. And the sight in the hospital of the children's limbs swollen with emptiness was not good; nor was the dread lest we should have delivered Jerusalem only to starve her to death. . . .

The shops were empty. There was no street and very little private lighting, for few householders could afford lamps, so that the city went to bed at sunset and, outside military formations, there was not one light to be seen in Jerusalem from the Mount of Olives; from which it was still possible to hear and to witness all the phases of the fight for Jericho. As late as 15 March fear of pestilence evoked the necessary (and most unpopular) public order forbidding the sale of old clothing or mattresses until they had been disinfected.

The fellah was a shivering bundle of rags. Beggars swarmed, and the eye, the ear and the nose were violently assaulted at every corner. With the help of the Army seven Sanitary Sections patrolled the streets daily, and it was made the duty of one man to keep the Via Dolorosa, from Pilate's Judgment Hall to the Holy Sepulchre, free from offence. The reek of the prison and the sight of the prisoners sentenced (if at all we knew not for what) and their misery froze the soul. . . .

As if these things were not enough, there were added to our troubles thousands of refugees. Over two thousand desperate Armenians besieged the saintly but incompetent locum tenens of the Armenian Patriarchiate.

I was sitting at my desk . . . when a Staff Captain broke in and announced that the Commander-in-Chief was walking up the stairs. It was my first sight of General Allenby, who had come with characteristically generous encouragement, "to thank me for taking charge." When he had questioned me as to the state of affairs he asked me if there was anything special I wanted, and I answered: "The food." Next morning and regularly henceforth lorryloads of wheat arrived without fail, and I breathed again.

Despised by All, 1918
T.E. Lawrence

The tale of Syria was not ended in this count of odd races and religions. Apart from the country-folk, the six great towns Jerusalem, Beyrout, Damascus, Homs, Hama, and Aleppo—were entities, each with its character, direction, and opinion. The southernmost, Jerusalem, was a squalid town, which every Semitic religion had made holy. Christians and Mohammedans came there on pilgrimage to the shrines of its past, and some Jews looked to it for the political future of their race. These united forces of the past and the future were so strong that the city almost failed to have a present. Its people, with rare exceptions, were characterless as hotel servants, living on the crowd of visitors passing through. Ideals of Arab nationality were far from them, though familiarity with the differences of Christians at their moment of most poignant sentience had led the classes of Jerusalem to despise us all.

The Writers

ARCULFUS (c. AD 670), known as Arculf, was a Gaulish
churchman, a bishop according to the Venerable Bede.
He visited the Holy Land shortly after the Islamic conquest in AD 637. He dictated his memoirs to a Scottish
clergyman after being shipwrecked on his way home.

WILLIAM HENRY BARTLETT (1809–54) was an English
watercolorist and printmaker, known mainly for his art
(many of the images in this book are from etchings of
his work), but the volumes he published following two
visits to the Holy Land intersperse the illustrations with
descriptions written from an artist's point of view.

97, 136 **GERTRUDE BELL** (1868–1926) was an English Arabist, traveler, political agent, and writer. Throughout her life she set new standards for the roles women were allowed to play in determining and executing Britain's policy in the Middle East; her *Syria, The Desert and the Sown* is still considered one of the best travel books ever written about Syria.

28 **RABBI BENJAMIN OF TUDELA** was a rabbi from Tudela in Spain, most of which was still under Muslim rule. He visited Jerusalem as part of a wide-ranging tour of the Mediterranean in 1187. He was principally concerned with enumerating his co-religionaries in each town and describing their condition.

54, 95, 132 **ESTELLE BLYTH** (1881–1983) was the daughter of, and sometime secretary to the Right Reverend George Francis Popham Blyth, the longtime Anglican Bishop of Jerusalem.

9 **THE BORDEAUX PILGRIM** In AD 332, a Christian pilgrim set out from his (probably) native Bordeaux to make his way across France, Italy, the Balkans, to Constantinople;

and from there to Jerusalem by way of Syria. His *Itinerary* is excruciatingly detailed about how many changes of horse, and so on, were required, but not vividly descriptive of what he actually saw. His account is the very earliest of any pilgrim: the city was essentially as it was when enhanced by Constantine, whose brother was joint consul and whose Church of the Holy Sepulcher was only six years old at the time.

Isabel Burton (1831–96) was the wife of British *91* explorer, adventurer, and translator (of the *1001 Nights*) Richard Burton. She was much more than just the wife of a celebrity, being an adventurous desert traveler, intimate of Arabic culture, and writer of vivid and witty memoirs.

Evliya Çelebi (1611–82) was a refined and educated Turk- *27, 84,* ish courtier and a devout but tolerant Muslim who traveled *107* all around the domains of the sultans as well as Germany and Hungary. His *Book of Travels* constitutes an extensive record of his experiences and of life in the seventeenth-century Ottoman Empire and neighboring Christian lands.

99   **FRANÇOIS-RENÉ DE CHATEAUBRIAND** (1768–1848) was a
French Romantic poet and novelist; he also wrote an influ-
ential defense of Christianity, *The Genius of Christianity*.

24   **ABOTT DANIEL (DANILO)** of Kiev was a Ukrainian *Igumen*
(clergyman) who traveled to Constantinople and the
Holy Land around 1106–1108.

116, 129   **JAMES FINN** (1806–72) was British Consul in Jerusalem
from 1846 to 1863. He and his wife Elizabeth Anne Finn
both wrote entertaining accounts of their sojourn.

38, 75   **GUSTAVE FLAUBERT** (1821–80) was one of the outstand-
ing French novelists of the nineteenth century; his
most famous works are *Madame Bovary* and *Sentimen-
tal Education*.

65, 73   **AMY FULLERTON** traveled throughout the Holy Land and
published *A Lady's Ride through Palestine and Syria* in
1872.

IBN BATTUTA, or Abu ʿAbdallah Muhammad ibn *78* ʿAbdallah al-Lawati at-Tangi ibn Batutah (1304–c. 1368) was a fourteenth-century Moroccan traveler whose *Rihla* (Travels) describes his extensive voyaging throughout the medieval Islamic as well as the non-Islamic world.

FLAVIUS JOSEPHUS was born in Jerusalem in about AD 37 *59* and lived through times that were as momentous in his native Palestine as elsewhere in the Roman world. His *The Antiquities of the Jews* gives a first-hand account of the state of things in Herodian (Second Temple) Jerusalem up to about AD 66.

KATHLEEN KENYON (1906–78) was one of the leading *6* archaeologists of her time, famously "digging up" Jericho and Jerusalem. Later in life she was Principal of St. Hugh's College, Oxford.

ALEXANDER WILLIAM KINGLAKE (1809–91) was an old *6, 113* Etonian who gave up the practice of law to travel. His account of his travels in the East (*'eothen'* means 'from the

East'), published in 1844, won him immediate fame. A terse style, keen powers of observation, and wry sense of humor make *Eothen* a masterpiece of the genre.

46 **ALPHONSE DE LAMARTINE** (1790–1869) was a French Romantic poet.

139 **T.E. LAWRENCE** "of Arabia" (1888–1935) was a British army officer who helped organize Arab resistance to the Ottomans in the Arab lands during the First World War, writing of his experiences and later disappointment in his masterful *Seven Pillars of Widsom*.

36, 72 **PIERRE LOTI** (1850–1923) was a French novelist, playwright, and (especially) travel writer with a taste for exotic situations and objects.

33 **HARRIET MARTINEAU** (1802–76) was an English social thinker and writer who spent an extended stay in the Levant and wrote up her impressions in the thoughtful memoir *Eastern Life*.

KARL MARX (1818–83), the author of *Das Kapital,* needs no introduction; while resident in England researching his magnum opus in the British Museum Reading Room, Marx padded his budget by contributing articles on European affairs to the *New York Daily Tribune,* which were often reprinted in other American papers. The excerpt cited is from a background piece to explain the "Oriental Question" behind the Crimean War, which was declared the week Marx wrote his article.

126

HENRY MAUNDRELL (1665–1701) was an Oxford academic and clergyman who spent several years in Aleppo as chaplain to the Levant Company. His dry wit and talent for vivid observation make his travel journal stand out from the predictable recitals of most of his contemporaries.

104

AL-MUQADDASI Shams al-Din al-Muqaddasi (c. AD 945–991) was a born and bred Jerusalemite, as well as a traveler. However, he took upon himself the task of describing his native city a little over a century before the

13, 80, 86, 115

Crusades. He was no provincial enthusiast, but a highly educated man who would write in the introduction to his memoirs, "I have spent my substance in journeyings, and have worn myself out in mercantile voyagings. And I have begun to write it only now after sojourning a long time in many lands." At home, he seems to have done well out of the pilgrim trade: "The Holy Land is truly a mine of profit both for This World and the Next."

15   **Nasir-i-Khusrau** (1004–1088) was a Persian pilgrim who traveled throughout the Middle East, visiting Jerusalem several times in AD 1017. His testimony is precious in that it was written before the Crusader sack and massacre of AD 1099, a violent regime change that lasted two centuries but left permanent scars on the cultural and emotional landscape of the area. He describes the monuments connected with the story of Jesus with reverence and even said his prayers next to the "cradle of Jesus."

109   **Grigorii Rasputin** (1869–1916) was a Russian clergyman and mystic who gained the confidence of the Tsar and

his family. Promising to heal the young Tsarevich of heredi-
tary haemophilia, Rasputin exercised a controversial degree
of influence over the Tsarina until his assassination.

Mary Eliza Rogers published *Domestic Life in Palestine*   *123*
in 1862. She spent eight years mostly in Haifa, with her
brother the British Vice-Consul, and had more intimate
familiarity with life in Palestine than most Victorian travel
writers, although the consular officials and their families
lived in a privileged and artificial diplomatic bubble.

Eduard or **Edouard Schuré** (1841–1929) was an Alsa-   *42*
tian (French) playwright, philosopher, and dabbler in
the occult.

St. Silvia of Aquitaine was a wealthy Roman citizen   *10*
from southwest France who traveled to the Holy Land in
the late fourth century. Her memoir gives precious testimony on the state of Christian worship at that early date:
for instance, hers is the first report of the use of incense
in Christian worship, or the celebration of Palm Sunday.

56, 137   **Sir Ronald Storrs** (1881–1955) was a British colonial administrator, serving as Military Governor of Cairo, Governor of Jerusalem, and Governor of Cyprus. His memoir *Orientations* is a valuable record of policy and personalities in the Middle East during and after the First World War.

48   **Catherine Tobin** (Lady Catherine Ellis Tobin) made two extended visits to the Levant, described in her 1863 memoir *Lands of Inheritance, Bible Scenes Revisited.*

52, 94   **Mark Twain** (1835–1910), the pseudonym of Samuel Clemens, is possibly in less need of an introduction than any other contributor; his wonderful record of his pilgrimage cruise to the Holy Land in *Innocents Abroad* is especially refreshing in its wry sense of humor that avoids the cynicism, gushing piety, or self-absorption that bedevil so many Victorian-era accounts.

119   **Bertha Spafford Vester** (1878–1968) was born in Chicago. Three years later, her parents, shaken by the deaths of four of their children in a shipwreck, went on a pious visit to the Holy Land and ended up spending the rest of their lives there, founding a millenarist religious settlement with a strong philanthropic mission. The hospital, now the Spafford Children's Center, still treats sick infants; the colony buildings evolved into the American Colony Hotel (still owned and managed by descendants of Bertha's parents).

Thomas "Buck" Whaley (1766–1800) was a well-connected Irish ne'er-do-well who squandered one fortune and lost another at cards; he went to Jerusalem on a bet that he could get there from Dublin and return within a year. He succeeded, pocketing £15,000 in winnings, but lost them forthwith. The exploit was immortalized in a popular ballad.

40, 70

Bibliography

Arculfus. *Pilgrimage in the Holy Land, about the Year 670*, Palestine Pilgrims Text Society Publications, vol. 3., London, 1895.

Bartlett, W.H. *Walks in and about the City of Jerusalem*, Hall, Virtue & Co., London, 1854.

Ibn Battuta. *The Travels of Ibn Battuta, Translated from the Abridged Arabic Manuscript Copies preserved in the Public Library of Cambridge*. By the Rev. Samuel Lee, B.D, for the Oriental Translation Committee, J. Murray, London, 1829.

Bell, Gertrude Lothian. *Syria, The Desert and the Sown*, Heineman, London, 1907.

Benjamin of Tudela, Rabbi. *Itinerary*, circa AD 1187, translated by M.N. Adler, Hakesheith, New York, 1907.

Blyth, Estelle. *When We Lived in Jerusalem*, John Murray, 1927.

The "Bordeaux Pilgrim." *Itinerary from Bordeaux to Jerusalem AD 330*, Palestine Pilgrims Text Society Publications, vol. 1., London, 1896.

Burton, Isabel. *The Inner Life of Syria, Palestine and the Holy Land*, 2 vols., Henry S. King & Co, London, 1875.

Çelebi, Evliya. *An Ottoman Traveller: Selections from the Book of Travels of Evliya Çelebi*, translation and commentary by Robert Dankoff and Sooyong Kim, Eland Books, London, 2011.

Chateaubriand, François-René (Vicomte) de. *Travels to Jerusalem and the Holy Land*, 3 vols., Henry Colburn, London, 1835.

Finn, James. *Stirring Times, or Records from Jerusalem Consular Chronicles*, 2 vols., Kegan Paul, London, 1878.

Flaubert, Gustave. *Oeuvres completes vol 10: Par les champs et par les grèves, Voyages et carnets de voyages* (Paris, Charpentier 1886); *The Complete Works of Gustave Flaubert...in Ten Volumes*, M. Walter Dunne, London, 1926.

Fullerton, Amy. *A Lady's Ride through Palestine and Syria*, SW Partridge & Co, London, 1872.

Josephus, Flavius. *Antiquities of the Jews*, trans. William Whiston. Project Gutenberg ebook, 2001.

Kenyon, Kathleen Mary. *Digging up Jerusalem*, Ernest Benn Ltd., London, 1974.

Kinglake, Alexander William. *Eothen*, J.M. Dent, London, 1908.

Krey, August. C., trans. *The First Crusade*, Princeton University Press, Princeton, NJ, 1921.

Lamartine, Alphonse de, *Travels in the East*, W. and R. Chambers, Edinburgh, 1839.

Lawrence, T.E. *Seven Pillars of Wisdom*, Jonathan Cape, London, 1937.

Loti, Pierre. *La Galilée*, Le Figaro, Paris, 1895.

L'Oyson, Emilie Jane Butterfield Meriman. *To Jerusalem through the Lands of Islam*, The Open Court Publishing Company, Chicago, 1905.

Martineau, Harriet. *Eastern Life, Present and Past*, 3 vols., Edward Moxon, London, 1848.

Marx, Karl. Article on the Oriental Question, *New York Daily Tribune*, April 14, 1854, p. 5 (written March 21, 1854).

Maundrell, Henry. *A Journey from Aleppo to Jerusalem at Easter A.D. 1697*, [Sheldonian] Theater, Oxford, 1703.

al-Muqaddasi, Palestine Pilgrims Text Society, London, 1891.

Murray's Handbook. *A Handbook for Travellers in Syria and Palestine,* John Murray, London, 1858.

Nasir-i-Khusrau, *A Journey through Syria and Palestine (1017 AD),* Palestine Pilgrims Text Society Publications, vol. 4, London, 1832–1918.

Von Noroff, Abraham, ed. *Pélérinage en Terre Sainte de l'Igoumène Russe Daniel, Au Commencement Du XII Siecle, 1113–1115.* St Petersburg, 1864; *The Pilgrimage of the Russian Abbot Daniel in the Holy Land 1106–1107 AD,* annotated by Col. Sir CW Wilson, Palestine Pilgrims Text Society Publications, vol. 4, issue 3, London, 1895.

Pliny the Elder, *Pliny's Natural History. In Thirty-seven Books,* translated by Philemon Holland, Barclay, London, 1847.

Rasputin, Grigorii. *My Pilgrimage to Jerusalem,* translated from the Russian by Todd Bledeau, Liberty Press, New York, 2013.

Rogers, Mary Eliza. *Domestic Life in Palestine,* Bell and Daldy, London, 1863.

Sandys, George. *A Relation of a Journey begun Anno Dom. 1610. Foure Bookes Containing a Description of the Turkish Empire of Aegypt, of the Holy Land, of the Remote Parts of Italy, and Lands Adioyning,* First Edition, W. Barrett, London, 1615.

Schuré, Edouard: *Sanctuaires d'Orient,* Perrin & Co, Paris, 1907.

Silvia of Aquitaine (Saint), *Pilgrimage of St Silvia of Aquitania to the Holy Places* circa 385 AD, Palestine Pilgrims Texts Society Publications, 1891.

Storrs, Sir Ronald, *Memoirs of Sir Ronald Storrs,* G.P. Putnam's Sons, New York, 1937.

Strabo, *The Geography (7 BC–23 AD).* Book XVI ii, 34–38; From http://www.jewishvirtuallibrary.org/jsource/History/strabo.html

Tobin, Catherine. *Shadows of the East,* Longman, Brown, Green and Longmans, London, 1855

————. *The Land of Inheritance; or Biblical Scenes Revisited*,
   B. Quaritch, London, 1863.

Twain, Mark (Samuel Clemens). *Innocents Abroad, or the New
   Pilgrim's Progress*, American Publishing Company, Hartford, CT,
   1871.

Vester, Bertha Spafford. *Our Jerusalem: An American Family in the
   Holy City 1881–1949*, Evans Brothers Ltd, London, 1950.

Whaley, Thomas. *Buck Whaley's Memoirs*, A. Moring, Ltd, London,
   1906.

Acknowledgments

The editors and publisher acknowledge with thanks the permission of Eland Publishing (www.travelbooks.co.uk) to use excerpts in this book from *An Ottoman Traveller: Selections from the Book of Travels of Evliya Çelebi*, translation and commentary by Robert Dankoff and Sooyong Kim, copyright © 2011 by Eland Publishing.

Special thanks to Nicholas Vester for sharing fascinating insights into his family's long history in the Holy City.

Illustration Sources

The illustrations in this volume are from: T. Hayter Lewis, *The Holy Places of Jerusalem* (London, John Murray, 1888): front cover (courtesy of the Rare Books and Special Collections Library of the American University in Cairo); George Sandys, *A Relation of a Journey begun Anno Dom. 1610. Foure Bookes Containing a Description of the Turkish Empire of Aegypt, of the Holy Land, of the Remote Parts of Italy, and Lands Adioyning* (London, W. Barrett, 1615): 1, 106; Wikicommons: 5; British Library MS Egerton 1070, *Les Heures de René d'Anjou*: 8; W.H. Bartlett, *Walks in and about the City of Jerusalem* (London, Virtue & Co., 1854): 12, 20, 23, 32, 37, 44, 51, 58, 64, 67, 75 (and back cover), 77, 103, 106, 111, 115, 125, 130, 135; Evliya Çelebi, *An Ottoman Traveller* (London, Eland Books, 2011): 81; Carl Werner: 86 (c. 1866); detail from "Entrance to the Citadel" by David Roberts, lithograph by Louis Hague: 90 (c. 1849); detail from "The Dome of the Rock" by David Roberts, lithograph by Louis Hague: 130.